For my parents,
who gave their everything to make my brothers and me into "Men for Others".
For my grandparents,
larger than life figures who are my inspiration.

To Chris,

the only thing we have to fear
is fear itself!

Thanks to:
My teachers, my brothers, Ian, Nevin, Phil, Justin, Gus, Dr. Clyde, Dr. Richard, Kathleen, Barnaby, Keith, Otilio, Hansel, Garrett, Barb, Sonia & Junneck, Frank & Patty, Nina, David, Anatoly, Irina, the WYSL family, Joe & his team at Ingram, and my aunt & uncle (for renting me an office).
Your advice shines through in this book.

Thanks to all my customers who gave me a chance when I was just a young guy with a briefcase and a little car.

Thanks to all my contributing editors for their invaluable insight:
Anthony C. Arena, author and medical coder
Kiran Babha, electrical engineer and business developer
Alan Brind, electrical engineer and business broker
Dr. Barbara Cottone, anesthesiologist
James Romeo, publishing expert
Paul F. Shanahan, Esq.
Steven Starowicz, electrical wire fabricator
James Starowitz, owner of starnova.com web hosting company
Cindy Wallace, teacher and photographer
Matthew Wallace, photographer and pilot

TABLE OF CONTENTS

Sections are in bold
Subsections are in italics

Chapter 1: Intro

"This book needed to be written. There's nothing else like it." - Anthony C. Arena, contributing editor

Intro

Hi. My name is Marc-Anthony Arena, and like you, I'm sick of technology. It's all upside-down. It's overblown, overdone, overkill, and is increasingly complicated. The industry is a constantly-changing pile of confusion/mystique/rumors, and as such, is a breeding ground for scams. I've dedicated my career to explaining technical concepts, exposing things that are less than honest, helping people feel less intimidated, and urging designers to make simpler products.

I have a knack for wrestling with computers and electronics for people. I grew up fascinated by technology, always excited to discover how things work. My dad's an electrician, and I started out taking apart old computers he'd bring home. I learned the fundamental concepts of his trade, as well as its need for industrial standards. My mom encouraged my academic pursuits, and my desire to bring order out of chaos.

Mix in one can of business degree, and let simmer for a few years. I'm now proud to have evolved into someone who can translate technology into Plain English.

I never cease to be amazed at how the technocrats take advantage of the fear they themselves foster. Confusing product design is always covered up as consumer ineptitude. The consumers are blamed, intimidated, and made to feel helpless, as the products become more and more confusing and greedy. I often think to myself, "How would this poor person ever set up this gadget without me?" There's no reason for this. *Technology doesn't have to be frustrating.*

I can't believe nobody has written a book like this yet. I'm going to expose the problems with this industry and educate you, rather than teach you how to cope with them. The ideas I'll discuss seem so obvious to me, but so often I see technicians who don't know them.

My career

Contrary to what you might think, my formal training in computers is not extensive. Aside from a few intro classes in high school and college, I'm completely self-taught, and am a self-proclaimed Level 7 Technician (as opposed to the Level 1s who read a script to you over the phone).

After college, I went through 5 years of doldrums, during which I greatly enhanced my skillset. I purchased a Mac Mini the day it became available, circa 2004. My Mac Mini was ultra-compact, minimalist, had the right features, and best of all, obliterated the 1980s fear that Apples "weren't compatible". It worked with any brand monitor, keyboard, mouse, hard drive, memory, it could read any photos or documents... openness at its best. One day, I broke its hard drive. I ordered a replacement online, but became impatient and bought another drive locally in the meantime.

Oh great, now I have a spare hard drive on my desk!

This spare part led me to start a side business where I bought used laptops on eBay that lacked parts. I would complete them and resell them as working units. I never made a fortune, but through a crazy chain of events, I ended up making contacts in the industry and was apprenticed by a local parts broker. There I honed my repair skills and and began to conceptualize the industry and its patterns.

I spent time as a lowly phone support agent for many companies. I witnessed customer service horrors and learned precisely what *not* to do, in both business and technology. I would answer tech support hotlines, and actually help people instead of blowing them off and telling them to run a virus scan (hence the Level 7 self-promotion).

Most of the issues presented to me could have been avoided if the users had simply rebooted their computers weekly, or purchased more reliable brands of equipment. Many tech support businesses are happy to make money fixing preventable issues, so far be it from them to teach prevention. I realized it'd be much more ethical and appealing to be the guy who fixes something once and for all.

Since age 9, friends and family have called me to help them with PC (personal computer) setups, TV connections, and even remote control batteries. I shuddered as senior citizens told me how they had to lug their heavy computers to local shops, leave them there for an indeterminate amount of time, and hope that their **user data** (stuff relevant to the user, such as your documents and photos) was still intact when they got it back. They'd have to bring it home and reconnect everything, including their routers and wireless printers, and live in fear of the next event. I knew there had to be a better way.

A friend of mine observed my ability to de-mystify tech concepts for people, and suggested I hang up my shingle. The career I'd been searching for was right under my Roman nose. I started Teknosophy, LLC as an IT (information technology) firm that performs on-site computer consulting for residential and home office customers.

Purpose

Over the years I've learned so much about how the residential IT industry is under-served. In your pool of local computer "geeks", half are condescending dudes who blame the general public for being "stupid". The other half mean well but charge customers *repeatedly* to fix constant *preventable* issues because they are unaware of the reliable technology that now exists. Then, of course there are the Big Box stores, whose employees seem to get 12 minutes of training. They hand your machine back to you after a long time, having erased your precious documents and photos in the process.

Very few will come to your home and solve the increasing number of connectivity issues that have nothing to do with your computer itself. The method I created is one where the technician makes your technology more stable and resilient to disaster, comes to your home and ensures everything is connected properly, and is an intermediary between you and the industry.

A shocking number of people on Earth toss their one-year-old PCs and laptops in the closet or the landfill. How could this be? Consumers using these PCs are scared into downloading fake "cleaner" or "optimizer" programs that claim to help. Those programs destroy the machine and beg for money. The consumers call their local computer guy, who then installs *more* useless cleaners, thinking he's helping the situation, but of course this makes it worse, so they think they're supposed to throw it away and buy a new one. Basically, the entire residential IT industry is a grease fire.

At this point, my head is bursting with ideas. I'm in a state of disbelief that no other book exposes the overall concepts behind this industry and solutions to chronic problems, such as fake cleaner removal or email synchronization. I'm eager to explain to the world what all these tech concepts mean and why your computer guy probably lacks experience. I'd like to expose why the greater digital world we rely on fails us so easily, because people need to know what's going on.

There are plenty of "how to use" books, but this isn't one of them. Rather, it's a book about the concepts, history, and politics behind the computer industry. The goal is to help consumers become more confident and informed. **You'll also learn how to save a fortune.** (Note all mentions of money in this book are measured in USD.)

Unlike many of the gadgets sold today, the concepts I discuss in this book are timeless. The examples I give may become dated, but my industry repeatedly makes the *same* design mistakes. Stupid design is eternal. Take "Why Software Sucks" by David Platt – sure it's from 2007, but the design mistakes he cites are still being made! He argues that using **software** (computer programs) sometimes feels like a minefield: You're always living in fear of pressing the wrong button and losing everything you just typed! Newer products have both an overabundance of buttons and are so good at destroying themselves, so users now feel as though they're walking on eggshells.

This book isn't written in expert jargon. This is a book written from an insider perspective, *in outsider's language.* My advisor David described this book as "the advice the experts give to their siblings" – which is a lot better than the worn-out "Here are some weird tricks your computer guy doesn't want you to know!". If you don't follow a topic, revisit it later, or don't worry about it! This book is meant to act as a guide for the 99% of people who don't want to become programmers, mechanics, IT maintenance people, or worry warts, just to get online.

Disclaimer: The views expressed in this book are the opinions of the author as an independent reviewer. The author is not liable for any actions you take to remedy your own situation!

Chapter 2: The Confusion Industry

"The future ain't what it used to be." -Larry Yogi Berra

The Chaos Industry

Consumer technology, much like economics, is a purely arbitrary, man-made science. During the dawn of computing, things improved incrementally. For a while, technology was becoming easier to use, but unfortunately in recent times the industry got carried away and the products they're designing have "a mind of their own". They think that *any* changes count as improvements, even if they complicate a situation or confuse the user. *Welcome to the era where the consumer's needs are ignored.*

As I watch customers use their own computers, I realize just how touchy these machines are! Right-click here, double-click here, but don't shift-wheel there... there are so many different ways to accomplish the same task, that doing one thing could cause you to accidentally trigger 300 unwanted results and never achieve what you wanted. (Ever try dragging a window a little bit? New machines "snap" the window to the top of the screen and maximize it for no particular reason.) It's like walking in a minefield! Congratulations, designers: You've done everything you could just because you could. Your overabundance of features has resulted in a delicate, brittle house of cards that falls with one wrong click. You've now instilled uncertainty and terror into the hearts of people whose lives are uncertain enough. This has discouraged exploration and confidence, and caused people to feel like they're walking on eggshells.

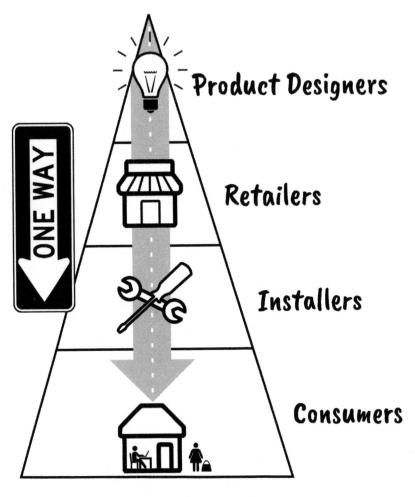

The clutter doesn't stop with the interface. When I walk through a retail store's PC section, I'm disgusted with the extreme number of advertisements I encounter on these brand new computers. (Unfortunately that's one of the few consistencies!) Each PC in the lineup has trillions of advertisements, scanners, and cleaners, and Windows itself contains a constant barrage of "action" items that ambush and confuse you with technical warnings while you're trying to get some work done.

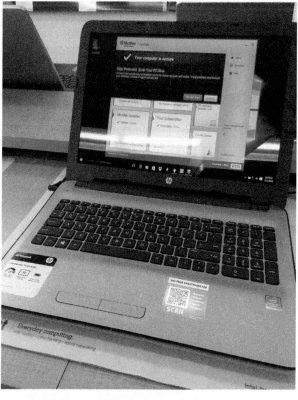

You also have some companies whose vision extends about two inches. These guys are creating products that either rely on the factory to function, or are only compatible with gizmos from the same brand. Many others are trying to charge you one time for a service, or rent you a single product.

Much of the industry is either incompetent or malicious. We're going spend a lot of time discussing how companies can ransack your computer and take your money, legally. Why bother writing viruses, when they can just call their program a Toolbar, Cleaner, Scanner, Optimizer, etc. and ruin people's computers for fun and profit? The typical **Fake Cleaner** or Fake Optimizer will start by advertising a website. It'll either claim that your computer is infected, or it'll appear as a big green "DOWNLOAD" button, hoping you'll click it instead of the one you actually needed. If you install it, it'll haunt your machine and attack at random: "HARDWARE ERROR! You have 90,000 COOKIES! Click here to register for the full version and do a scan to fix it!" Not only is this pile of buzzwords ineffective against physical damage or speed issues, but you may think your computer itself is displaying the message, when in reality it is the scammer trying to pilfer from you legally. Many IT professionals are still unable to identify these as threats.

Every day, more and more and more and more half-baked, disposable products are created. There appears to be a complete disconnect between the majority of users and this runaway train of an industry. *Since when did this become acceptable?* Much of my work is encountering brand new items that don't work right, and then putting the finishing touches on them so they're actually usable. We're increasingly dependent on technology. People's digital lives are becoming almost as important as their health or spiritual lives. It's crucial that the people we trust with our data know what they're doing and can keep it intact. I'm hyper-focused on making people's digital lives simple and solid.

This chapter is going to introduce you to some of the nasty things that are going on right now, and later on we'll discuss them in detail, including how to avoid or remedy them!

Better Living Through Chem... er, Software

Do you remember playing the game Jenga as a kid? You started out with a tower of wood blocks, tightly packed. Players would take turns carefully extracting one block from the tower and placing it on top of the tower. With each move, it would become taller but much less stable.

Many products today are designed in the same way. Some product designers confuse quality with features. Rather than designing a more stable program, they might stick a "crash recovery wizard" into a program. It's easier to add features than it is to stabilize the ones you already have. It's also more pleasing to the marketing department.

The more features a product is designed to have, the more likely that it will be unreliable.

Products used to be well-made and simple to use. Think 1950s appliances, 1990s Japanese cars, or modern high-end audio products such as those from NAD and PSB. **Focus on simplicity and quality.**

Poor product designers eschew a solid experience in favor of an increasing number of anti-features. These kinds of products are cheaper to produce, they sound better on paper, and break more easily so the consumer has to keep purchasing new ones. Think inkjet printers, or over-engineered German cars.

Anti-Consistent, Anti-Intuitive, Constantly Changing

You'll hear me coin a lot of terms like these throughout the book. Sure, in most cases change and upgrades are a good thing. In the 90s, technology became more "user-friendly", in other words, *logical, familiar, and consistent.* Somewhere along the line, though, the designers and marketers became addicted to change and the sales revenue that comes with it. Designers often change things for absolutely no reason, resulting in horrified and helpless customers. Unfortunately, we're at a point where many products aren't even finished! They're just rough drafts known as Beta versions... *Welcome to the world of eternal Beta products.*

Technology changes so fast, people and even repair guys can't catch up. That's why the gag gift known as the "DVD Rewinder" sold so well!

More and more things are being made with software because it's so changeable – but it's like building houses out of mashed potatoes. Contrary to what people say, computers are the least logical things ever. How often does your stuff work right?

Consider the story of Microsoft's recent mega-flop, Windows 8. They took their perennial Windows product, left its overgrown 30-year-old core largely untouched, and removed the Start menu we had been accustomed to since 1995. Next, they super-glued a completely separate product onto it, which featured colored squares flying around that displayed advertisements and the user's private photos. (They were sued for trademark infringement when they named the separate product Metro, so I refer to it as Evil Colored Square Mode.) The result: The most confusing product ever created by human hands. Average users are *still* unsure of how to access their documents and programs! Unfamiliar, unintuitive, disrespectful. Conversely, Apple made a smart move when it overhauled the core of its Operating System in 2001, but preserved the user experience.

According to Computerworld magazine, only about half the Windows 8 machines unleashed on the world were active on the Internet only 15 months later.[49] Experts estimate the other half of those machines were either smashed, thrown outside, tossed into closets, left unsold, hit with a destructive update, or erased and upgraded with alternative software.

Living in this industry is all about *fear and misconception.* I've heard countless stories of customers buying a secondary computer that is left disconnected from the Internet, or running a regimen of malware scans because somebody thought it might help them. Again, eggshells.

Newer ≠ Better

Computer guys worship the word "newer". They believe that just because something came out after its predecessor, it's automatically better in every way. Rather than using solid design, their only remedy is applying a software patch (basically a chunk of bubble gum) to a product or replacing it with a new one. The restless designers *intend* to tweak a product, but oftentimes get carried away: They may remedy one issue and cause three more. A recent dark turn of events has product designers begging customers to download an update every few minutes.

While many new technologies (e.g. SATA hard drives, the USB port) have helped streamline computer hardware, others are *worse* than their predecessors. A great example is HDMI cords. In the past, we used many different cables (VGA, DVI, composite, component) to connect televisions and computers to their accessories. That's all been replaced by the HDMI cord, but HDMI has a hidden tradeoff that makes it arguably worse than the prior cables. Sure, it streamlines your mess of cables and offers stunning quality, but unbeknownst to many, it also includes a futile anti-piracy technology that is the reason behind all those crashes and interruptions in your movie. If you ask Big Box Store employees about it, they will swear "HDMI is better in every way, because newer always means better".

Think of it another way: Just because someone invented something (you know, like bell bottoms, Coke II, aspartame, or the 1980s Mustang) do you think that gives them the right to smash any prior products and force the new ones down people's throats?

Stable is better. Simpler is better. Better is better. Newer is not always better.

Vendor Lock-In

In the 80s and 90s, Sony TVs were considered the best. Why? Because they lasted a very long time, bore a prestigious design, worked well with other products, and the user interface was obsessively consistent between models. They succeeded by competing and being the best. Their own company history declares: "[o]ne company should not monopolize a market even in such a small country as Japan. Markets would be stimulated by the presence of many competing companies."[36]

Now, however, it's a different story. Rather than competing, companies are now bent on forcing you to be dependent on them. They want you to become a part of their *ecosystem*, having to buy their TVs, their computers, their music devices, and so on. The theory goes like this: If Acme makes their devices compatible ONLY with Acme devices, then in theory *you'll have to go out and buy everything from Acme*. Acme television, Acme computer, Acme toaster, Acme toothbrush, Acme underwear. In the computer industry, this vertical integration is called **vendor lock-in**.

In more recent history, Sony was the poster child for this stove-touching behavior. Everyone knows the story of Betamax: In the 1980s, Sony invented a technically better standard for video tapes, but they wanted to hog all the revenue to themselves, thus limiting other manufacturers' ability to adopt the standard. They eventually opened up and allowed Toshiba and others to create Betamax VCRs, but it was too late. There were also MiniDisc, LocationFreeTV, ReaderStore eBook readers.... all well-made products that flopped colossally because they were proprietary.

This is because many marketingbobbleheads believe creating a monopoly is the goal. They're not satisfied with doing the best they can on a level playing field, so they end up eating 100% of their own tiny, short-sighted pie. They implement proprietary technologies because they don't understand that this discourages adoption of their products.

The goal here is to pigeonhole someone into buying all components and accessories from one company forever, which inevitably backfires for all involved. We must be very wary of such greed and short-sightedness.

Think of vendor lock-in as an abusive relationship – *I'm all you need, there's nothing out there for you, stay here and put up with me.* I for one would rather have a client (or girlfriend!) who actually loved me, than one who was forced to be with me. If someone at your company proposes such a scheme, fire them.

An inevitable downside: If you're a company that has a captive audience, why bother improving or responding to their needs? Where else are they going to go? One of my favorite things to do is liberate people from such closed systems onto more flexible platforms.

Avoiding proprietary platforms in favor of global standards allows a consumer to change his allegiances more easily. Don't forget, at one point each city or country kept its own time and its own system of weights and measures. Eventually we had to get onto Standard Time Zones and the Metric system so we could visit and trade with each other. During the dawn of television, each brand envisioned the use of its cameras, antennas, and televisions. Luckily the NTSC/PAL/SECAM television standards were agreed upon, so any brand of television could watch any program. You'd think that would be obvious from day one, but greed tries to get the best of young industries. Unfortunately, the computer (and Smart TV) industry hasn't figured this out yet. Hopefully they will once they read this book.

Platforms

For better or worse, it's much easier to create a product *for* a platform than it is to create your *own original* platform. That's why we see so many PCs based on Windows, tablets based on Android, games housed inside Facebook, and **blogs** (online journals) hosted on major blogging sites.

EpicMealTime (a Canadian cooking show where drunk bachelors prepare lasagnas made out of hundreds of fast-food burgers) or their countryman Justin Bieber are two great examples. They started out as kids with cameras and ended up worldwide celebrities, made possible only recently by **distribution platforms** such as YouTube.

My company created a product based on Android for only a few thousand dollars, which would have cost a few *hundred* thousand if made from scratch. The same is true for boutique sports car manufacturers: They don't bother to develop their own engines. Pagani, Spyker, and Lotus buy their engines from established sources such as Mercedes, Audi, and Toyota. Ideally, we would love to create something original, but we have to start somewhere.

When this idea is taken to an extreme, we are in danger of stagnation. In some segments, new competitors could easily come in, but computer guys are both lazy and a bit too enamored with using preexisting platforms. *747? Concorde? Space shuttle? Why bother when somebody already invented this perfectly good Zeppelin!* Hence, the computer industry sloths itself into in-bred de facto monopolies like Windows, eBay, QuickBooks, and Photoshop.

It doesn't help that many consumers prefer the devil they know rather than seeking out more stable alternatives.

Monopolistic Competition

I adore small neighborhood Chinese takeout places. It's fun to stop in, order something delicious, and enjoy a Saturday night dinner eating at the coffee table watching Kung Fu.

Why are these places so fascinating? Most of them have great prices and tasty food, but what's striking to me is, they all offer a familiar experience while remaining completely independent. I'm sure they attend conventions to meet food distributors and pick up this year's bikini calendar, but there is no need for a central ego charting the industry's course. No central authority mandates that your favorite corner takeout place must serve dish 7, 9, or 11 (but as always, ✎ denotes spicy).

In macroeconomics, this is known as monopolistic competition. These restaurants, like farmers, all offer a similar and interchangeable product, and are competing purely on price and quality. (Chinese low-end electronics companies will even compete with products *based on the same blueprint!*[83]) Such a model, in my opinion, is stronger than a centralized one. A tall tower may fall, but a group of houses don't collapse all at once.

The computer industry could learn something from all that. In the 1990s, each online dial-up service wanted to become a monopoly. Companies like Prodigy, Compuserve, and AOL wanted to be your "walled garden." Each one had exclusive content, and allowed you to communicate only with fellow members of the same services. Each one wanted to take over the world. They were all eventually superseded by the Internet, which (like telephones and the postal service) was neutral and universally compatible.

Unfortunately, some greedy pioneers still haven't learned this lesson.

What is the Cloud, anyway?

Let's put this on the table first: **The Cloud** simply means outsourcing your data to an online service. That's it. The name originated in the 1990s when nerds at business meetings would depict the Internet as a cloud when they drew whiteboard diagrams.

Think of it as a mini-storage garage or a gym locker. In that way, it's fantastic: I rent space on a cloud server for the documents I'm currently working on, so I don't have to work in my office! Yes, I can and do run my business from anywhere in the world. I can connect to my private company websites wherever I am and view my customer database, collaborative calendar, training manuals, and invoicing systems. I can use virtual phone numbers from Google Voice and MagicJack, so I can use my office phone number wherever I am.

All these liberating services have made it easier than ever to start a business, and manage it from afar. (Vacationers now have to make an effort to "unplug" and enjoy the weather!) Outsourcing to all sorts of different cloud services grants small businesses the powers previously only available to large ones. I can even type a book and submit it instantly to a publisher of my choice, who can print single copies of the book when someone orders it! No more having too many or too few on hand. I can print business cards, sell and ship products around the world, accept credit cards, and do many other things that used to be hurdles for small businesses.

However, being in a connected world means you're also connected to potential intruders. We've all heard news stories of how Chinese hackers have taken the Social Security numbers of the US Federal Government's employees. In 2016 we found out how secure Hillary Clinton's Microsoft Exchange server was.[84]

Ignoring or unaware of such risks, the tech sector is chasing the "cloud" gravy train like a dog chases a car. They think that everything should be cloud-controlled from now on (regardless of whether or not it makes sense) forever and ever, Amen. In my opinion, it's just hype – something that may be great in certain situations but is not meant for everything. Unfortunately, it's now being forced on us by the makers of some newer Operating Systems. Microsoft's Windows 10 "guides" people into creating a single cloud account that controls access to all of their devices. Now, a malicious program or hijacker may be able to gain control of *all* of your devices in one fell swoop!

Bet you didn't know this: When Apple shoehorned the Sierra update into people's machines in 2016, Sierra started taking people's documents and sucking them into the iCloud Drive service. (iCloud is Apple's name for its form of cloud services.) Sure, it was probably in the fine print somewhere, but how many customers are aware that this is happening? As an added bonus: If you have multiple Apple machines, documents from one machine start spewing onto your other machines![61] Do you think this is in line with Apple's mission of an elegant, simple experience?

If you're a Microsoft Office user, do you know whether your documents are stored in your computer, or in its OneDrive service? *Oh I'm sorry, did you want to keep your private documents and photos in your computer? Did you want to have control over where your stuff goes?*

Cloud services are like public places: Sure, we want to go out and do things in public, but we probably want to keep our most important private possessions in our own homes. When the dust settles, we may discover that some things are done better on the cloud, and some things are definitely not.

Be very wary of cloud services that offer one-way migration. They're all too eager to take your data, but make sure they're willing to give it back if you ask for it.

Over-centralization

In Soviet Russia, citizens depended on a single municipal hot water heater for their showers. How often do you think that worked properly? Russians now enjoy in-home hot water heaters as a modern luxury.

Have you noticed all of these new gadgets, be it tablets, phones, and smart fridges, or voice-controlled devices, are all dependent on the cloud, in other words, on a faraway central computer? While it certainly helps in some circumstances, a lot of companies are getting slap-happy with centralized control. In the event that a cloud service shuts down or an update goes awry, you're left stranded with no recourse.

Computer guys and their marketingbobblehead coworkers sometimes show a deficiency of common sense or logic. As convenient as centralized products and services are, the downside is, now more than ever companies want to control the products they've sold you. There is a new wave of completely factory-tethered products, whose fallout includes:

- Customers feeling increasingly helpless
- Customers unable to choose what to do with their own products
- Rigidity: Autonomous cars and other devices now have baked-in logic that's unmodifiable by consumers
- Landfills full of factory-dependent products that become paperweights the day the factory goes under

An example of this is the impending tidal wave known as **IoT** (Internet of Things). These are "smart" household devices that are connected to the Internet, so that you (and hackers, and big business, and big government) can control your appliances without having to be in your house.

Cars and computers are merging onto the same highway, pun intended. In their infancy, both were originally a bit too hard to use, so owners had to become mechanics. Now, both require less maintenance but are less user-serviceable and less modifiable. They want to sell you a product that relies on the factory. Unfortunately, the result is, these things that are so crucial to us are managed in the most impersonal way, based in some faraway data center.

We should learn a lesson from history here. Thousands of years ago, The Library of Alexandria was the central place for human knowledge. When it was destroyed, with it went unfathomable amounts of knowledge. If a cloud company fails today, all of the information held in it is likely gone, too.

In the "How it All Works" chapter, we'll discuss why **Open Source** is so important. Open Source is software written by volunteers, released as public domain, for the betterment of humanity. Not only are Open Source products more stable (think Firefox or LibreOffice), but they're completely independent and customizable.

The automotive industry, once a haven for American ingenuity and empowering customizations, is so desperate for revenue that it's striving to prevent customers from repairing or customizing their own property! They're now claiming that modifying or even *repairing* your vehicle is verboten, because they own the rights to the closed-source software lurking inside your car.[50]

My fear is that this new unmodifiable world will create a barrier to entry for DIYers and pioneers looking to start new and fresh things. In contrast to all the greed, Open Source is an up-and-coming movement that aims to keep the world running a little more smoothly. As auto review site Jalopnik puts it, "True luxury means freedom."[34]

The End of Marketing

My industry effectively believes marketing is now obsolete. In a centralized industry, why bother convincing people of your new product when you can just insert it into their machines?

Many software products nowadays employ an intimidation tactic I call **update attacks**. Software publishers believe they can change or patch the products you own, whenever they feel like it, all under the guise of making the product more secure. Update attacks come from legitimate companies (or impostors of them). Anytime a message urges you to install something to improve your device, especially if it screams "Now or 5 minutes from now?" or offers no clear way to opt out, that should throw up a huge red flag. More on this in a bit.

It's not just limited to companies you already work with. In the case of **toolbars** (evil legal programs that hijack your homepage and screen space, then intercept your Web searches), the computer industry feels as though they can force people to be their customers, rather than having to go through all that trouble of actually having to convince them.

Since it's become harder to back up your photos from your smartphone to your computer manually, the industry is all too eager to "help out". TechCrunch reported on a recent App called Everalbum that offers to hold backups of the photos on your phone. It asks for your contact list, then spews messages to all your friends, leading them to believe you've shared an album with them! It then signs them up, asks for their contact lists, and spews messages to their friends, ad infinitum.

Organic (grassroots) growth wasn't good enough for that company. They wanted it right away, and they didn't care to spend the time convincing people why they should sign up.[67] Unfortunately I believe this is the attitude of much of the industry.

The Failure Ecosystem

There are multibillion dollar industries to support the recurring failures present in products such as those from Xerox and Microsoft. In other words, the products require constant maintenance from day one, which then creates a whole ecosystem of "repair guys" who go out and repair the same issues for people over and over. I've discovered that these recurring issues are preventable by switching to more solid products. That's the foundation of my business.

What many "computer guys" fail to see is, true success and customer admiration come from removing the preventable issues, and replacing them with products that do not contain these shortcomings. This is why my company focuses on delivering post-Microsoft technologies and post-POP email accounts wherever possible.

Some of us may remember the Maytag commercials of yore. "The Maytag Repairman: The loneliest guy in town" went against this "repair industry" mentality. Eventually, more and more products (such as the iPad, or the Mint OS) will emerge to shatter the unnecessary ecosystem.

It's like the Broken Window Fallacy – When someone breaks a glass window, this "stimulus package" causes society to expend money and time fixing something that used to be perfectly fine. This means they have less time and money to spend on other things that needed attention. When people tell me I'm lucky that my industry is in such demand, I tell them it's economically inefficient to keep repairing computers over and over when there are plenty more real problems we could be solving, like world hunger.

Printing Money

The inkjet printer industry has a death-grip on the average Joe's wallet. I routinely meet customers paying $50/month for ink cartridges *engineered to die,* satisfying the industry's thirst for an inky river of revenue. HP is crafty enough to offer a monthly subscription for ink (replete with a tiny discount), so you feel better about the fortune you're giving them.[23] This is a perfect example of how the IT industry is getting away with selling products that are worse than their predecessors only because the public isn't aware of an alternative. Few consumers are aware that laser printers cost about the same, are cheaper to operate, and have legendary reliability. We'll spend some time teaching you how to protect yourself from the printer industry.

The Current Experts

In the land of the blind, one-eyed men are kings. Remember Y2K? We couldn't predict what percentage of computers would malfunction the night of Dec 31, 1999. I for one expected the power to go out, at the very least. Sure, there were good guys out there doing simulations on crucial computers to ensure they'd still be running when the ball dropped, but the world was replete with half-wit ding-dongs lookin' to make a buck. If you were one of them, you could fabricate a story and write your own ticket.

Unfortunately, the continued shortage of good technicians means people tend to trust anybody who can type fast and look smart. Such technicians either only know how to *use* the machine, or attempt to maintain a machine by employing virus/malware scanners that seek out extinct threats. Because the industry changes so rapidly, they oftentimes lack the instinct to go after anything sinister they encounter on a machine, such as a fake cleaner program.

Most technicians mean well, but the industry is 99% misinformation, misconception, confusion, mystique, and rumor. Ever since the 1990s, when I hear someone say "My uncle's neighbor's cat's third cousin's pastor's friend's dog's grandma's nephew is a computer expert and he recommends..." I know it's going to be another zinger.

I got into the fray not for the money, but because I didn't see anybody doing the job right. If one of my customers becomes impatient and calls a competitor, I'm upset because eventually I'll have to clean up after some newbie's destruction. Much of the time, these guys simply erase the customer's computer, without bothering to preserve any of their documents or photos. *Oops! Oh well!*

Bulls in a China Shop

I define superstition as an unproven yet widely-held belief that a certain action causes an outcome. You know, knocking on wood, doing a rain dance, that sort of thing. People do it but it's never been proven to help. Such is the case with virus scans and cookie-flushing that's going on nowadays. Many computer repair folks perform scans and updates when the issue may be caused by an impostor program or a faulty circuit board!

Many local shops offer new PCs, malware removal, printer repair, custom programs, and design websites too. These are all completely different disciplines that should be handled by different specialists. Unless of course you enjoy going to your dentist when you need cataract or foot surgery!

Your typical "computer guy" might be arrogant, condescending, or perhaps smelly. Some enjoy recurring revenue, either by renting commission-based products to the unwitting or by actually believing that you need monthly maintenance on a home computer. He wants his customers to depend on him for maintenance and even password storage. A huge number of them install pirated copies of Windows because they're not trained on how to install Windows in accordance with the legal license that came with your machine. Inevitably, at some point every computer guy vanishes to another galaxy and is never heard from again.

After he disappears, his customers are left in the lurch. The next day, those customers ask their friends for a recommendation, and they end up giving me a shot and experiencing my radical approach.

The Helpless Desk

People also call me constantly and state that they've spent 8 hours on the phone with their gizmo's manufacturer and received zero help. *What, you expect the manufacturer to have reps who actually know their own products?*

One customer recently spent two hours on the phone with tech support because every time they tried to burn a CD, it would fail halfway through. Inevitably those hours were spent trying the most asinine and irrelevant solutions, such as virus scans or browser updates. (The answer, of course, is a bad CD/DVD drive, a mechanical part that cannot be replaced via phonecall.) Imagine calling roadside assistance while stranded with a flat tire, then spending the next 6 hours pouring windshield washer fluid in your gas tank because the dispatcher told you to! After finishing this book, you'll know more than most tech support folks for sure.

Gizmodo reported one of the many horror stories about an inept support agent spreading myths:

> I got a call about the product being slow. His quote was this "The electrons on a mother board can be slow sometimes because of the angle of the computer. Is your computer leaning?" I know this not because I heard what he said, but because one of the floor managers happened to be monitoring his call and ran out of her office "STOP STOP STOP" and took over the call. We all died laughing.[51]

Internet Speed Issues

Many people, senior citizens and otherwise, are fooled into paying for technology they don't need. (How much of the computer industry's revenue is earned unnecessarily?)

I've encountered zillions of customers who are paying for an extremely fast Internet connection, yet have constant speed and reliability issues. All they wanted to do in the first place is some very simple web browsing and emailing. Here are some common scenarios:

Scenario 1: New Customer

1. Customer calls the **ISP** (Internet Service Provider) to sign up for service.
2. Agent answers the phone and reads a questionnaire from a script. "What sort of things do you do on the Internet?"
3. Customer answers something like "Internet, email, and video streaming."
4. Agent sells the poor customer an extremely expensive Internet package.

What's actually happening

Here's the rub: Almost anything the customer says triggers the requirement for a high-end connection. If they say they do online banking in addition to ordinary tasks, the fact that they said "online banking" requires the employee to recommend an extremely fast, overkill connection. Since many helpless desk employees have zero understanding of the Internet, they follow the script blindly, or make up outlandish things like "If you have a basic connection, the waves in the wires would be too weak for WiFi (wireless Internet)."

The truth is, for basic web browsing and even watching Netflix, a single person would be perfectly fine with a 2 Megabit connection (usually confused with "megabytes" by phone support folks). Yes, it's fully capable of WiFi.

If you call and complain about the price, their script tells them to say something like, "Well yeah, but that's how we got you the best value for your money!" - Sure it may be the best value for the money, but it's more than enough for a city block. Some of the creepier agents even look at what types of services you've been using and tell you that those services may not work anymore!

Scenario 2: PC Speed vs Internet Speed

1. Customer's individual computer is slow, because some "Internet Security" program or fake cleaner is slowing it down.
2. Customer calls the provider to complain of speed issues.
3. Agent assumes the customer needs a heartier Internet connection. Agent offers to increase the Internet connection speed coming to the house.
4. Customer pays more money for the Internet, and the problem isn't solved in the least bit.

What's actually happening

What many consumers and technicians fail to realize is, the speed at which your computer does math has nothing to do with your Internet connection.

The helpless desk might not know the difference between computer speed and Internet speed, but they'll gladly sign you up for a more expensive Internet connection as a first resort.

Scenario 3: Slow or Unreliable Service

1. The Internet connection coming into the house is solid, but the customer experience is slow or unreliable.
2. Customer calls provider to complain of Internet speed issues.
3. Agent assumes the customer needs a heartier Internet connection. Agent

offers to increase the Internet connection speed coming to the house.
4. Customer pays more money for the Internet, and the problem isn't solved in the least bit.

What's actually happening

What if you called your local Water Authority and told them you have a broken kitchen faucet? If they offer to increase water pressure in the pipeline to your house, that doesn't fix your issue, does it?

The answer is this: The customer was simply using the wrong equipment. They were infected with a combo box.

Recently, most ISPs have been renting people **combo boxes**. A combo box is a combination of a modem and a router, and it does both jobs poorly. (Like that screwdriverflashlighttoastershovel thing from TV shopping networks.) Because it only works if you're less than, say, 20 feet away, everyone in the universe who has a combo box has problems. As one Arstechnica forum user puts it, "But mine sucks, my neighbor's sucks, my coworker's sucks, my cashier's sucks, and my other neighbor's sucks."[59]

You could have the most fantastic Internet connection in the world, but if you have a combo box, that's your bottleneck.

The Solution

What boggles my mind is the level of misconception in my industry that causes scenarios like these. Since consumers *and* phone support folks have no basic education of the big-picture concepts, grave troubleshooting errors are committed, and unintended consequences occur.

In all these scenarios, I'd clean the individual PC and replace the combo box bottleneck with a real router and modem, so you actually get the speeds you pay for. In many cases, the customer can then call and request a reduction of Internet service – at that point, the speed reduction is not noticed, but the savings are!

(You've got this problem too, huh? We'll discuss how to solve it in the Combo Box section.)

Small Businesses

Tech Support

I've heard horror stories of small businesses paying $1,000/month for:
- Java Updates
- Adobe Flash Updates
- Virus Scans

...all of which are automatic anyway. Careful, folks. Chances are these machines are simply polluted with toolbars after employees went to coupon-cutting websites.

Customer Relationship Management

Small businesses need software programs that are made for their industries. Each industry is beholden to its own garbage software program, usually written by some tyrant in a basement in the early 1990s. You can either put up with this ancient monopoly, or pay big bucks for a modern custom PHP system (please do), or you can look to rent a cloud package.

Here's the advantage to a cloud-centric business software package: Paying a subscription fee ensures you don't have any on-site data to worry about, and you can call the helpless desk all month long. If you're going to depend on a software product familiar with your industry, make sure it's a modern one.

The disadvantages are these: Your user data is no longer at your office. This means it's physically located in some other building, somewhere. Unless you're making proper, readable local backups of your database, *you're at the mercy of that vendor's existence.*

The next thing is this – every cloud service uses *its own* database system. This implies that it's virtually impossible to switch vendors, or horribly difficult at best. If that firm goes out of business, you'd have to have a database engineer perform a forensic extract of your information and create a new, custom product for you.

The feeling of *complete helplessness* that comes with over-centralization manifests itself here. I was at a local shipping franchise one day, and the "new" shipping software sent by the central office was barely functional. The employees were resigned to the fact that it didn't work, and went back to using the old package. Most small business software is designed poorly, never tested, and lacks user feedback.

Websites

I cringe when I hear people say they have a website for their small business, because chances are they were scammed. I've heard horror stories:

- The more scummy web developers will oftentimes OWN your domain name (such as www.JaneDoeCatering.com). So, when they go to another galaxy and stop answering their phone, the website name *you thought you owned* is now dead and out of your control.
- Some guys will charge $7,000 for a cookie-cutter site. They then wipe the sweat off their brows and tell you they did hard work.
- There is a large company out there that preys on small business owners who aren't tech savvy. Some charge $987 per MONTH for a Kindergarten-level website, and attempt to keep the customer under contract for years.
- Other companies mail people letters when their website domains are about to expire. What they do is tap into public information that your name is expiring, attempt to impersonate your current vendor, and then dupe you into signing up with them! You ASSUME that the company that sent you the letter is your domain hosting company, so you sign on the dotted line and mail them a check. At that point, the scammers own your website.

WiFi

Many cable companies are now offering "Free WiFi" to restaurants and other small businesses, for their patrons to enjoy. That's nice of them! However, the customer cannot use it unless they prove that they're a paying customer of XYZ Cable Company. It's kind of like me walking in and saying, "Hey, you can only give out that free garlic bread to Teknosophy customers!"

Naturally, the only small business owners who have permitted this are the ones who aren't aware that they can purchase their own wireless router and offer Internet service to anyone they darn well please.

Backup Hard Drive Myths

Many or most people have no backups of the user data on their computers. So, if their hard drive dies, they lose all of their documents, photos, music, and so on. (Most big-box computer technicians are unaware that user's data is important, so they oftentimes erase a customer's computer and hand it back to them without even thinking about it.) What's worse, many people buy a backup hard drive and are coddled into thinking the hard drive will automatically know what to back up.

Myth 1: "Automated backup hard drives help you. Just leave it plugged in and let it do the work!"
- Not quite. Most automated backup programs just dump the contents of your hard drive onto a backup drive with zero regard to what's actually relevant. You might only have 1 GB worth of user data, but an automated backup might bloat your backup drive with hundreds of GB of backups of your corrupted Windows folder and programs, which are impossible to restore

anyway. (Imagine buying a new house, taking your old leaky basement with you, and leaving your possessions behind!) This unintended consequence leads average people to buy many huge backup drives, thinking they have excessive amounts of information.

- Most automated backups are also not human-verifiable. Connect your backup drive to a new empty computer and find out if you can actually see the contents of the backup drive. You probably won't be able to, because most automated backup systems hide your documents in billions of sub folders based on the date they felt like backing them up.
- Many automated backup drives use a proprietary program that only works on Windows, and only on the current version of Windows you have. So, if you're attacked by a Windows Update, or if you have to buy a new computer, the automated restoration function may be unusable.
- Leaving any hard drive plugged in to your computer opens you up to hazards. If you're hit by a cryptolocker (explained later) or maybe a lightning storm, you've lost everything.

Myth 2: "Having photos on your computer slows you down, so keep all your stuff on an external drive"

- Many jokers think that this is the case, when in reality having items on your hard drive can never slow you down. They have no idea that the only things that can slow a computer down are daemons.
- If you take your user data away from your computer and keep it exclusively on a backup drive, guess what? Inevitably, your external drive dies, and you've lost everything. Your computer guy didn't understand the concept that you must keep your stuff in *two places at once*.

Later on we'll discuss how to perform a real proper backup that'll store your data in a more efficient, human-verifiable, universally-compatible fashion, so it'll be recoverable on any brand of computer you buy.

Email Pandemonium

Believe it or not, some people still use POP email – a technology dating back to 1988.[15] If you're infected with POP email, symptoms include:

- Duplicate emails showing up on your tablet and computer
- Having to delete the same email on all the devices you own
- Zero email synchronization between your tablet and your computer
- Having to periodically "unclog" your mailbox by logging in to a website
- Zero backup in the event your computer dies
- Zero spam (junk mail) protection in most cases

Does this sound like you? While it's shocking to me, many people are still experiencing this chaos. POP nightmares leave no demographic unharmed: Many important businesspeople with crucial emails just think this is how the world works, and perhaps their IT staff or Internet Service Provider is unaware that other options exist. I've developed a magical process to migrate you to a modern email address *without losing past or future messages*. Stay tuned for that.

My Customers

"Hi Marc, I'm Jane Doe. I need you because I use a computer at work and at home, but I don't know much about technology. I feel intimidated, I don't know what virus scanners to use, my last computer guy was condescending and said I was stupid. He was beamed up to another planet and I haven't heard from him since. I don't do a lot, but my computer is horribly slow, takes 10 minutes to boot up, and is flooded with popups. It's a whole year old so I need to know what computer to buy next year. So I've resorted to using my little smartphone as my computer and I do everything on it. I have all my photos on there as well, but can't import them to my computer because my photo library keeps duplicating itself!"

I get phonecalls just like this every week. In reality, these are people of above average intelligence: teachers, lawyers, business owners, even an actual brain surgeon. Are they to blame? NO! Technology is oftentimes designed by slobs who are either short-sighted, lazy, or obsessed with features.

People end up using their tiny smartphones as their computers simply because they're non-Microsoft, but in reality they'd love to have their widescreen computers back in action. Those phones of course hold tons of photos that aren't being backed up properly as well!

Users who know what they're doing

There are plenty of tech school grads and professionals who *do* know what they're doing. Their computers work fine most of the time, so they assume that the average Joe is simply stupid and lacks the skills to perform computer maintenance.

They might not realize *so* many people are being *so* badly scammed, by evil companies and unstoppable hostageware that evade virus scans. The secret isn't how often a user scans for viruses – it's the fact that experienced users simply don't click on things that try to lure them in, such as the fake driver updater ads and the "Warning! You have 1,000 trojans!" pages.

Of course, there are also IT professionals who are honest and capable. After reading this book, you'll know how to identify them!

Placebos

There are plenty of security measures out there that help you feel warm and fuzzy, but in reality do not protect you. What's worse, they tend to slow you down, corrupt your system, and some even beg you for money.

This is a castle. It appears to be secured and well-guarded, but in reality bad guys can walk right in, since there's a hole in the back. I've had my illustrator show you this because it describes my industry so well. The general public follows the security superstitions the industry prescribes, yet the bad guys still come right on in.

This situation occurs in so many different scenarios, from email provider hacks that took over the accounts of 1.5 billion Yahoo users (all of whom sat at home doing virus scans, thinking it was helping), to **Support Scammers** who claim to be computer experts and walk right into your computer and wallet. You'll recall this diagram quite a bit with many of the examples we discuss.

UAC

One example is Microsoft's **User Account Control** (commonly known as User Annoyance Control) which is built into newer versions of Windows. Every few minutes, UAC darkens your screen, plays a loud ***BOING!*** and asks you if you'd like to

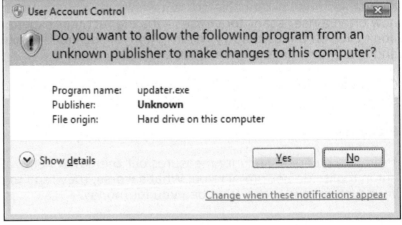

perform some scary technical operation. Its original purpose was to prevent bad guys from sneaking in by prompting you before the system made major changes. However, since most new threats are either unstoppable or legal, this can *only* serve to overwhelm and annoy. You can turn it off in Control Panel under Users.

Complex Passwords

Oh, passwords. Short-sighted nerds will tell you to make your passwords as crazy and contrived as you can, and then change each one often. According to them, the more you worry about your password, the safer you'll be! (Unfortunately some of the more brutal websites will force you to have numbers, exclamation marks, perhaps some music notes, Zodiac signs, and Chinese characters too. The complexity requirement GUARANTEES that people forget their passwords.)

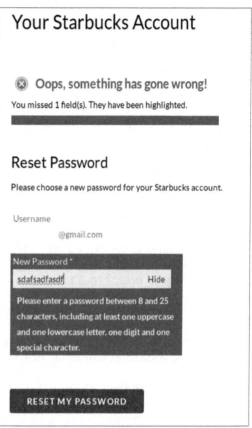

- If you work in a large corporation, you'll have 15, 20, or 30 different usernames+passwords. Many worker bees are required to change each one every 30 days, resulting in utter chaos. (IT contractor companies *love* that because they are paid for every password reset they perform!)
- The end result is, people end up resetting their passwords every time they have to log in to something (or sometimes signing up for a whole new account unknowingly). Because professionals have to reset their passwords so often, many of them stick with the defaults of "password" or "Welcome1". If that's not it, their passwords are written on Post-It notes all over their desks.

If you have an account that's been stolen, it was probably cracked by:
- phishing (more on that later)
- a computer that doesn't know the difference between a Roman letter and an special character (to a computer, a character is a character)
- or someone who walked in the back door of your provider and just took everything (this happened to Yahoo)

Believe it or not, many of my customers think you don't even need a password to get into things! The day they bought their computers 900 years ago, their kids/computerguy/cellphonestoreguy allowed their computer/phone to remember their passwords. Every time they buy a new device, they think they're supposed to just create new accounts for everything. Much of my business comes from helping people recover their passwords and keep them all straight. *Never* trust that your computer or password manager program will remember your passwords, because it *will* lose them at some point.

Keeping your myriad passwords all written on a real sheet of paper in a safe place at home eliminates the constant forgetting/resetting cycle. Guard this sheet of paper with your life.

Oh yea, and when checking out at an online retailer, try using Guest Checkout. Then you don't have to remember another password, they won't spam you for the rest of your life, and if someone breaks into their computers, they won't learn as much about you.

My Approach

I've devised a whole approach based on doing the opposite of what the prevailing industry opinion is. This has come to me through many, many painful lessons, which help me learn and grow. Unlike most other guys in the industry, I train technicians so as not to limit them to one brand or product set. I empower my technicians to absorb knowledge of any product on the spot, to see the big picture, and thus to *adapt* to all the new problems we see every day. This is because we think creatively when solving a new problem, and realize it's just a new manifestation of some prior skulduggery. Rather than know a rote set of procedures in a manual, we learn the concepts, so even if the version or the product changes, we can still understand what's happening. (Just as your mechanic knows what an oil filter is, regardless of what brand car your bring in!)

I come at this from the perspective of the consumer, as opposed to from the perspective of the tech support guy on the other side of the transaction. As opposed to condescending talk and cookie-cutter answers, I remind the customer not to feel bad, and that all my customers are doctors, lawyers, business owners, or otherwise intelligent people who are artificially intimidated by technology. Products are becoming harder to use *because* they're more complex. I ALWAYS seek to find a minimalist solution tailored to the needs of each beginner/intermediate customer. Setting them up with a set of SIMPLE products that work RELIABLY is revolutionary in this industry.

My hope, and my bet, is that integrity always prevails.

Chapter 3: Concepts & Threats

"He that hath no rule over his own spirit is like a city that is broken down, and without walls." - Proverbs 25:28, KJV

Your PC takes 20 minutes to turn on in the morning and is afflicted with nonstop pop-ups. You assume you have a virus. It's two years old, and you think you're ready for a new one. Not so fast! That's not the case at all. In this chapter we'll discover why everything in the entire IT industry is upside-down.

I teach an adult ed class called "How to Protect Yourself from Your Computer". The typical student is in my target market – Baby Boomers who are otherwise intelligent but intimidated by technology. They all walk in with the same exact scenario, and usually feel ashamed because their computer guy berates them for not running enough virus scans.

The course isn't HOW to use a machine, but rather to:
- reveal the concepts behind computers in an easily-digestible manner,
- discuss the various categories of threats that exist in the computer world,
- and describe which companies are doing what new things in the industry.

We then take a normal average PC (which I've screwed up on purpose before the class) and run my trademark cleanup on it. There students discover the trouble had nothing to do with viruses or age at all, and I uncover the real reason behind the machine's slowness: **The New Threats**.

Finally, I give a basic overview of how the Internet works (a truly fun learning experience) and discuss a few more concepts. The idea is to help people feel enlightened, empower them to fortify their digital lives, and remove all the feelings of intimidation and terror. So, without further ado... my adult ed course in a nutshell:

The Platforms

Let's begin by explaining platforms. Consider this: If you were born in France, you speak French, you read French books, you watch French TV, and so on. If you were born in Italy, you speak Italian, read Italian books, and so on. There are a few things, though, that are universal around Europe: You can drive the same cars, pay with the same currency, and display the same hand gestures at drivers you don't like.

The same thing goes for the computer industry. We're going to learn about the three major desktop/laptop platforms:
- Microsoft Windows
- Apple Macintosh
- and Linux

Likewise, in the smartphone/tablet arena, the three major platforms are:
- Apple's iOS
- Google's Android (spoiler: it's based on Linux)
- Microsoft's Windows Phone CE? 8? 10?... whatever they're calling it this week

Owners of Microsoft Windows PCs must purchase software and accessories (printers, scanners, webcams) that are compatible with it. Owners of Apple Macintoshes must purchase software and accessories compatible with that platform, and so on.

Luckily, an increasing number of products are **platform agnostic**, meaning they were:
- created for, and tested to work with, all three of the major platforms (most printers nowadays)
- or better yet, simply designed using global industrial standards that all platforms obey. For example, most digital cameras create JPEG photos, which all platforms can read, so when new PCs and OSes are released, no testing is needed!)

As you may have guessed, platform agnostic stuff is the way to go.

The Traditional Personal Computer: What all the parts do

People always call me flustered when trying to discern what new computer is right for them. What I tell them is: *Specifications don't matter anymore. Even the cheapest new computer is more powerful and capacious than a normal consumer would ever need.* In most cases, there's no need for anything more than a cheap machine.

Avoid **cloudbooks**, as they're a bit too spartan. They're really only useful in elementary schools and hotel lobbies. Of course, you'll also want to avoid any brands that prove to be unreliable. Ask your friends how long their HP laptops lasted.

If you've ever wondered how your computer works, here you go...

The inside of a standard PC

Random Access Memory, aka RAM

This is a stick of memory, also known as **random access memory (RAM).** Contrary to popular belief, it is not where your files are stored. RAM is a short-term storage area for your computer to do its work. Think of it as scratch paper during a math test, or a cocktail napkin where you write down your latest brilliant idea. The more RAM space a computer has available to it, the more efficiently and quickly it will work. When you restart/reboot your computer, the RAM is flushed clean. This does not affect your files, such as documents or photos.

The Hard Drive

Your hard drive is where everything is actually stored. Think of your hard drive as the long-term memory in your brain. It contains **three key groups**:

Your **Operating System**	
The main piece of software on your computer that allows you to run programs. Examples of OSes are Windows, Mac OSX, and Mint.	
Your **Programs**	
Word, Excel, QuickBooks, Call of Duty, The Sims, etc.	
Your **User Data**	
Known as your User or Home folder. This includes all the files relevant to you: Documents, Pictures, Music, Downloads, Videos, etc. (If there are multiple people in your home, each person can have his own Home Folder.)	

Hard drive storage is measured in Gigabytes. Most new machines come with 500GB drives. If a salesman is pushing you to buy bigger, consider this: I have been collecting music and vacation photos for 20 years, and have thousands of documents (which don't take up much space). All this adds up to only 150GB.

Standard hard drives are small metallic discs that spin around (most at 5400 or 7200 RPM). There's a needle, similar to that of a record player, that reads and writes information to the disc.

New hard drives called **SSDs** (solid state drives) store information on chips, so there are no needles. They're wicked fast, and last just as long, but cost a few bucks more.

Again, your hard drive carries three categories of information (OS, Programs, User Data). Note that **ANY HARD DRIVE OF ANY BRAND OR STYLE CAN DIE AT ANY TIME.** Both regular and SSD drives are incredibly difficult to repair, so if yours dies, chances are you've lost that data forever. (That's why it's so important to have proper backups!)

The CPU

The **Central Processing Unit** (aka CPU or processor) is a powerful calculator made of silicon. When you balance your checkbook, it may take you five minutes to perform a few mathematical operations. A 2.3 Gigahertz processor, however, can handle 2.3 *billion* operations per second. We haven't managed to make a silicon processor much faster than 4 GHz, which is why you see machines advertised with two or four cores. This simply means multiple CPUs are stuck together, like a tandem bicycle.

The two major manufacturers of processors for desktops and laptops are the American firms Intel and AMD. Mobile devices (smartphones and tablets) are based on architecture from ARM, located in the UK.

The Power Supply

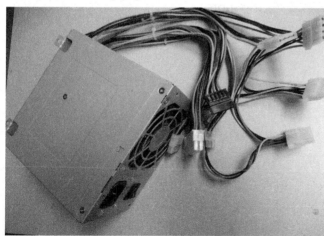

The power supply takes electricity from your wall and distributes digestible portions of it to the components inside your computer/laptop. (Sort of like a bird chewing up worms for her babies!)

The Motherboard

The **motherboard** is the main circuit board that ties it all together. When the power button is pressed, it wakes up and says:

Hey, what am I? Oh I'm a motherboard!
Okay, CPU and RAM, are you present? Great.
Video? Great.
Hey Mr. Hard Drive, do we have an Operating System?
Cool, let's do this!

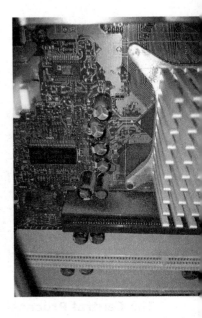

The Optical Drive

This allows your computer to read and write to CDs and DVDs, using a laser. You can thus enjoy your favorite album or movie on your computer. When buying a laptop, be aware that some do not include optical drives anymore.

Peripherals

Of course, your machine is connected to a variety of accessories: Keyboard, mouse, printer, microphone, and perhaps others, such as a webcam for face-to-face conversations.

Bonus concept: Driver

A **Driver** is a small piece of software that teaches your Operating System how to deal with your particular accessory, such as a printer or webcam. On a modern computer, most of the time the OS deals with drivers for you, so you should never have to deal with them.

Beware! There are fake driver updater programs out there that promise to keep your drivers up to date, when in reality they simply bully you for money, and slow your machine down. Drivers rarely need to be updated, but most users and Level 1 techs don't know this. Imagine a door to door salesman offering to update the studs in your wall, for only $1000 per month! The only time you really need to deal with them is during construction or during a remodel.

Mobile Hardware

So there you have it. Those are all the components you'll find in a typical PC or laptop. Believe it or not, tablets and smartphones have almost all of that – but it's all on one small circuit board! Unfortunately that means if your mobile device dies, you should find a trustworthy recycler, because your information's still inside that circuit board.

The types of malware

I define malware (malicious software) as this: A piece of software that
- Nags you
- Spies on you
  and/or...
- Slows you down

That being said, let's take a look at the types of traditional malware that are out there.

Conventional viruses

Many computer guys believe viruses are the only type of threat out there. Viruses are simply malicious computer programs that are instructed to spread from PC to PC and wreak some sort of havoc. The purpose is to give the creator some "street cred," like, "Hey I just wrote a virus that shut down that power plant and a bank!" or "Hey I just wrote a virus that spread around the world and made the evening news!"

Trojans

Trojans are similar. If you read that boring book *The Iliad*, a Trojan Horse was a vessel filled with invading soldiers, disguised as a gift statue. A trojan is simply a virus that presents itself to your computer as a gift. While these don't occur super often anymore, **stowaway** software is the same concept, but it comes in legally because it sneaks in underneath other products.

Email Worms

There are countless examples of Microsoft Outlook (and its old sidekick Outlook Express) spreading email worms.[69] Oh yeah, once in a while people use it to read email as well.

Email worms are simply viruses that spread themselves through email. They can read Outlook's address book easily and send themselves to your friends! Unfortunately, most large organizations still see Outlook as an acceptable email reader tool, despite the constant discovery of security holes. At any rate, as long as you avoid Outlook (not to be confused with the unrelated Outlook.com service) you probably won't get worms.

More fun facts about Outlook while we're at it:
- It can actually slow down your entire machine if you have thousands of emails. As an added bonus, it destroys itself over time.
- It has such an overabundance of useless anti-features (here's lookin' at you, inexplicable Flagged Status Column Mode), that someone should offer a Master's degree in it. If you use it at work, you've played Whac-A-Mole with those features as they enable themselves.
- Outlook rolls all of your emails into a ball known as a PST. If one speck of it corrupts itself, the entire ball goes out of alignment and you've lost all your emails, the whole shootin' match.
- If you're still stuck with its offspring Outlook Express, chances are your computer's been hijacked and reprogrammed as a *Spam Zombie:* In other words, it's being used to redistribute Viagra emails around the world on behalf of some spam lord.
- I enjoy replacing it with a safe, nimble, easier product called Thunderbird.

Rootkits

Rootkits are simply malware that hide in the "basement" of your computer, waiting to strike when the time is right. Most rootkits manifest themselves in your web browser during searches: Imagine searching Google for pizzerias in your town. When you click on, say, *Little Venice*, it redirects you to the rootkit publisher's site, such as "get-fast-search-results-now.com" which then redirects you somewhere else. What's the point of that? Well, that *somewhere else* is usually a legal websites that pays referral bonuses to anyone who brings them traffic. Got it?

Spyware

Spyware is the general term for software that lurks in your computer, monitors your behavior, and reports it to someone. Early spyware threats, such as Gator or GAIM have been eradicated, but unfortunately this strain has mutated into a new, legal form. Stay tuned.

Remember...

These definitions aren't precise. The computer world is an ambiguous, myth-laden one that experiences rapid change. Also note that for the most part, for all intents and purposes, that traditional malware & viruses can only harm Microsoft Windows machines.

Yes, post-Microsoft machines have flaws too, but the chances of being hit with one of these traditional threats during normal usage are astronomically rare: One of the few times a Mac has ever caught a virus was in a laboratory setting[77], likely with a Mac whose defenses were compromised by Java technology.

Many nerds claimed that Microsoft products are simply targeted because of their popularity, and that once Apple products became popular, they too would be vulnerable to attack. People got away with that myth until the day when half of all Internet traffic came from Apple phones,[37] and we realized those products are still relatively invincible. Think of it this way: I can have 10 houses made out of brick or I can have 100 houses made out of brick: No matter how many I have, they're still stronger than the ones made out of straw or sticks.

Plenty of people are targeting the new non-Microsoft products, but they have to use other methods such as tricking the user emotionally (**social engineering**). There are two threats using this method that we'll discuss in a bit. The first makes you think you're giving your password to someone legitimate, and the second leads you to believe your tablet/smartphone/Mac/toaster/toilet is vulnerable or infected. (Spoiler alert: It's not infected, but someone is trying to convince you that the fake virus scan they just ran on your totally healthy machine is worth $1000.)

Ironically, I've heard stories of clowns at local cell phone stores and office supply stores who are totally unaware of these new scams. They're convinced by the scam that you have viruses, so they panic and and oftentimes end up erasing your phone/computer and all your precious photos and documents.

Myths and Buzzwords

Let's shatter the rest of your misconceptions:

Musket Scanners

In the "old days" of the early 2000s, good people made anti-virus programs to combat viruses, which were written by bad guys in faraway basements. Viruses were behind all the mischief back then, but now, that's really not the case. Viruses aren't happening nearly as often as The New Threats...

Recently, anti-virus programs have grown into bloated "Internet Security" suites that slow you down by around 90%, provide constant "High CPU Usage" warnings (their fault), and protect you from very little. It's like installing an autoimmune disease or a paranoia disorder on your computer. It oftentimes prevents you from doing things you want to do, such as emailing or printing. What these vendors don't want you to know is, Windows Defender (née Security Essentials) is free from Microsoft and comes inside every new PC!

Anecdotally, I can tell you, I see a traditional virus maybe 5 times a year! Most cases I deal with are caused by one of The New Threats such as toolbars and phone scams, an update that roasted a machine, or an Internet Security suite gone awry. Unbeknownst to your local computer guy, virus scans cannot help you against these threats.

When explaining the futility of anti-virus products in this modern age of scams, I equate it to an airport security check. If they pat you down and only look for muskets, wooden clubs, or bows and arrows, how safe are we?

Malware/Spyware Scanners

There are plenty of people out there who run 4, 5, 6, 7, or 8 different malware scanners, usually because some computer pundit told them to. **Many of those same people end up buying a new computer every year, thinking that mysterious gremlins break their hardware, when ironically, their machines are totally fine, hindered only by the scanners!** Many of those scanners were effective 15 years ago, but are now comparable to flyswatters at a swordfight. If you're *that* bored on Saturday nights and are itching to scan something, then the only one I recommend is **AdwCleaner** because it goes after toolbars and fake cleaners, without having to haunt your computer on a daily basis. As always, watch for impostors.

Home WiFi Security

Before I forget, let's talk about home WiFi (wireless Internet). I've gotten calls from people who are alarmed that they can see their neighbors' wireless router names on their computers. Once they see this, they conclude that their neighbors can see their wireless name, and assume it means their neighbors can see what they're doing on their computers! Not to worry: Just because you can see your neighbors' WiFi router names, and just because they can see yours, doesn't mean a thing.

You can all see each other's front doors as well, but it doesn't mean you can walk into someone's house without a key. As long as you have a password on your WiFi, nobody can use it without the password. Even if you give your house guests your password, they can only use it to get on the Internet while visiting you. It doesn't automatically grant them access to the contents of your computer. Don't worry!

Registry cleaners

Remember, one could define a scam as convincing someone they have a problem when none exists. They then present a "solution" to your "problem", which involves you paying them.

Another perennial favorite of the industry is the registry cleaner. Most programs that claim to clean your registry are like snake oil products that just haunt your machine, slowing it down and displaying innocuous statistics in an attempt to convince you there's a problem.

If you really want to know what the registry is: When you install a program into your computer, not only is the folder placed in your hard drive, but it then intertwines its tentacles into your copy of Windows. Think of getting a new job or a new relationship – there's a lot you must integrate into your routine. The original intention of the registry cleaner was to remove leftover references to programs you no longer have, theoretically allowing your computer to worry about less things.

So here's the deal: The registry is a rat's nest. I've seen PLENTY of situations where a registry cleaner inadvertently destroys someone's copy of Windows.

Cookies

On New Year's Eve in Aruba, you can hear firecrackers blowing up in the streets all day long. This is a traditional way to ward off evil spirits, that spells fun and traffic jams throughout the island.

Unfortunately, some computer guys are just as haphazard. If you talk to an average computer guy, you'd think **cookies** were toxic pollution! If a computer guy or TV ad claims that cookies are slowing down your computer, it's an indicator that they have no clue what they're talking about. It's a scapegoat, akin to your mechanic claiming that the bugs on your windshield are the reason why your car broke down.

Cookies are simply small files stored on your computer that contain information about what pages you've seen or what products you viewed on retail sites. These allow websites to display advertisements relevant to what you've been doing lately. For example, if I'm browsing for watches on Amazon, a while later an ad will come up that'll invite me back to watch shopping, even displaying some of the watches I've reviewed.

The European Union is so flared up about them that all websites are now mandated to warn people about cookies. In reality, they're just digital barnacles. They don't slow you down or ruin your life, and they aren't nearly as damaging as things like toolbars. It's just a buzzword that's used to scare you.

There are plenty of fake cleaner programs that claim to wipe your cookies for you, but they usually bring in a few pieces of stowaway spyware when you install them. If you really feel like cleaning them out, you can do so easily in your web browser. *Disabling cookies altogether isn't a great idea though,* because online banking and other legitimate sites rely on them in order to work properly.

Firewalls

First off, here's what a **firewall** is *not*:

- active protection, like a scanner
- something you need to install
- something that can prevent scams, such as those that try to scare you into calling them for "tech support"
- whatever your computer guy told you it was
- magical

A firewall is a *passive filter* that helps stop crank callers from sending commands to your computer or network. Whenever a bad guy tries to send a command to your computer, the command is ignored. That's it.

Up until 2002, Windows machines accepted any and all remote commands. This was great for high school teachers, who could send shutdown commands to the entire classroom at the end of class. However, when connected to the Internet, your machine could be controlled by anyone, anywhere.

Why firewall software is useless

If you buy a firewall software program for your computer, it will only serve to waste your time and money, and give you plenty of false alarms that will eventually cause your computer to become so paranoid, it stops communicating entirely.

Every home router *already* contains a firewall that protects the computers and devices within. Moreover, even if you're in a public place such as a café, any computer that's made after ~2002 *already* contains its own software firewall. If your computer asks you if you're in a public place when connecting to WiFi, answer honestly and it'll heighten its vigilance for nearby pranksters until you get back home. (Therefore, if you can't print wirelessly while at home, oftentimes that means you accidentally told your computer you were in public, and it became suspicious of your printer!)

That's it.

Defragging

I loved my college roommates, but they were slobs. They would come home every day with bags and bags of DVDs, bicycle parts, and toy guns, and pour them out onto the floor before skipping off to class. During long weekends, yours truly would alphabetize the DVDs and put them on the shelf, then take the other sundry pieces and organize them in small piles in front of each person's bedroom door.

There you go, now you know what **defragging** is! When your computer takes in new photos, music, and programs, it throws the files around the living room floor. Defragging simply organizes them so the computer can find them more easily.

Why defragging is useless
  * Sure, it may improve your speed by a fraction of a percent, **but the real villains are the legal spyware and bloatware.**
  * Many "computer guys" don't realize Windows comes with its own defrag utility. They end up search for third-party Fake Cleaner-style defraggers online... which will bring 50 toolbars in with them and ironically make the PC slow as molasses.
  * Defragging takes hours. If you have that kind of time, volunteer at a soup kitchen.
  * It's not even possible to defrag a Mac or a Mint machines because they're so efficient to begin with.

Free Games

I tell customers, if they like seeing me often, they can either lure me with Italian cookies... or let their kids use their main household computer. While kids may be more confident in using computers, the "dirtiest" computers I see are always those used by kids.

They go on Google and are lured in by anything that says free games. Kids always end up at free computer game websites and free television show websites (all shows listed are pirated). On such sites, scammers disguise themselves as free versions of Minecraft or as Adobe updates. Inevitably, the kids will click the huge colorful DOWNLOAD button. Such folks end up infected with piggyback programs such as toolbars, or things like the Torch browser, a mutilated version of Google Chrome that allegedly sneaks in and offers music piracy features. Do a web search for "Torch browser" and the results describe its questionable nature.

Take a breath

Did all that just blow your mind? The next time you see an "average computer guy" offer virus scanning services to help your computer stay fast and safe, you'll shudder like I do, realizing he hasn't had training in 10 to 20 years.

What's a consumer to do?

Other Scams

Phishing

In a **phishing** situation, you receive a fake email claiming to be someone else. Like this:
- "Hi, we're probably Chase Bank. And you probably need to click here because someone probably did something to your account..."
- or...
- "Hi, we're probably DHL, and you probably have an important package. (You were expecting one, weren't you?) Click here to get your tracking number..."

Then... boom. You're brought to 1 of 3 different kinds of sites:
1. A site set up to try and sell you diet pills or Viagra.
2. A site that injects hostageware/ransomware/cryptolocker into your computer, especially if you're afflicted with Internet Explorer (more on this later).
3. Most commonly, phishing scams will put up a website that *impersonates your bank or shipping company*. It's much easier than people realize to create this. All one has to do is save the logo graphics from the real company's page, and then create a simple website displaying those graphics.

On this fake site, there will be boxes for your username and password. At that point, you'll type in the username and password you normally use, and it'll suck it in and save it. It'll then give you a "sorry wrong username/password" message, which then causes you to... yup, try another password. And then another. And another, until you've given the scammers all your usual passwords, which they'll gladly sell or use against you.

Do not log in to a site unless you're absolutely sure you're at the official site. In order to make certain, follow these two tips:

- When you see a "click here!" link in an email, *hover your mouse over it.* In the next several seconds, the ACTUAL destination of the link will be revealed. If it says something like "scummyscammersite.com/amazon.com/login", then you know to stay away from them.
- If you do end up clicking on the link, check the spelling of the website. I've seen many sites like 3bay.com or paypa1.com, or scammer.com/ebay.com/index.html. In order to make absolutely certain, check to see that the site begins with http**s** and a green lock should appear in the address bar. Clicking on that lock should reveal a security certificate that assures you you're at the official site:

- Alternatively, you could also just NOT click on any links. They're all useless.
  - If it's an email from your bank, call your local branch on the phone to see if they actually wanted to tell you something.
  - If you are expecting a legitimate tracking number from a shipper, you *never* need to click on any links in emails. Write the tracking number down or copy-paste it – and if they don't include one, that's your first sign it's a fake.

Since traditional viruses are virtually impossible in this post-Microsoft world (Have you ever known a Mac user who got a traditional virus?), bad guys have to find a new way to get into people's stuff. What better way than to use fake security warnings? Be extremely wary of any email or text message or that tries to scare you. There's a chance they're actually hunting, er, phishing, for your password.

Nigerian-style, a.k.a. 419 scams

In **419 scams**, someone claiming to be Nigerian (in actuality they could be anywhere) either declares you inherited money, or that they're interested in buying your car/house.

The cover story usually begins stating their niece/nephew is delayed in Lagos but, since they've heard you're a good/nice/fun/godly person, they're interested in partnering with you. Once they get you to agree to a transaction, they mail you a fake check or money order, written in a higher amount than expected. They then tell you to mail a slightly lesser amount to one of their friends, and tell you to keep the change. Your bank later discovers their check was fake, but it's too late - by that time, their friend cashed your good check and has your money.

Here's what a typical 419 scammer letter looks like:

Subject: Dear Respected One

Dear Respected One,

IT IS WITH GREETINGS IN THE LORD THAT I GREET YOU. I HAVE HERAD THAT YOU ARE AN HONEST AND GOOD PERSON. MY NAME IS MR. MBUNTU MBUNTU I AM THE DAUGHTER OF THE LATE MR. AND MRS. ASDFJKLF MBUNTU. THEY WERE BANANA GROWERS OF GREAT WEALTH. AFTER TRAGIC AIRPLANE EVENT, THEY HAVE DISCOVERED TO HAVE NO NEXT OF KIN (INHERITOR). THE TOTAL SUM IS OF. $103 MILLIONS USD DOLLARDS. IF NO KIN IS FOUND, THE MONEY WILL GO INTO CUSTODY OF THE COURTS. WE ARE LOOKING FOR A PARTNER TO TRANSFER FUNDS TO YOUR COUNTRY.

I HONOURABLY SEEK INTEREST IN YOUR NAME TO ASSIST ME IN SEEKING TO COLLECT THIS FORTUNE. IF YOU SHOULD ASSIST IN CLAIMING THE MONEY BEFORE IT IS HELD BY COURTS, I WILL GIVE YOU A PERCENTAGE (%) OF FORTUNE FOR YOUR TROUBLES IN YOUR HONOURED TIME. MY NEPHEW IS INDEED IN LAGOS, HE IS A DOCTOR, AND IS IN FULL CUSTODY OF THIS TRANSACTION. AWARENESS.

WE WILL NOT USE THIS MONEY FOR ANYTHING AGAINST IN THE BIBLE. PLEASE FOR PRIVACY CONCERNS REASONS EMAIL ME TO REPLY AT:
totallydifferentemail@hotmail.com

WHAT ALL DUE REGARDS.
MR. MBUNTU MBUNTU

If you're bored at work, and have already read every Chuck Norris joke the Internet had to offer, there are many websites out there that offer hilarious collections of "greatest hits" 419 scam emails. If you receive one yourself, it's also fun to waste their time. See how long you can lead them on!

Google Local Scams

A handful of fly-by-night companies call every number on planet Earth, misleading people into thinking they're Google. They'll say things like, "This is a notice, that your Google Local listing is not up to date!", which causes ordinary people to hate Google, thinking it's them calling!

Here's what's ACTUALLY happening: Legally established (evil) companies try to convince computer-illiterate folks that their businesses aren't on Google and "for only $500 per month, we'll pay Google so you can be on the Internet!"

Don't Bundle Up

Here is one of the most important concepts of the book that many computer guys and most consumers don't know: A good bit of the programs you download are poisonous. If you search for a product like Firefox or LibreOffice, you'll often land on an impostor page. They'll say in microscopic letters something like "Oh, by the way we're not actually the official website." or "If you download this, it'll come with a free Download Manager!" They'll then give you the product you wanted, usually packaged with a **software bundler** that allows their sponsors constant unfettered access to install stowaway malware into your machine.

Stowaways are precisely what they sound like: Evil malicious software programs that sneak in underneath things you download, *but it's all perfectly legal because you clicked OK.* It's technically legal, because you technically installed the software willingly, assuming you read the entire license agreement, and assuming you're a computer expert who doesn't mind being at the wrong site and taking in some stowaways. IN REALITY, though, this filth is unwanted and affects many, many people from all walks of life, who believed they were at the official website.

Download OpenOffice Completely Free!

Download OpenOffice today and get access to the world's favorite open source office suite.

Don't pay for Microsoft Office or any other office suite when you can download OpenOffice for FREE! Save $679.95 by downloading OpenOffice today.

Open Office Can:

Create text files, spreadsheets, presentations

Manage databases

Edit images

Open all Microsoft Office formats

Save files as PDFs

Save you a lot of money

 Download the complete Open Office Suite for Windows now.
Compatible with Windows 2000, XP, Vista or 7 (64 and 32 bit). Click here for other operating systems.

Clicking this Download button starts DownloadAdmin™, it manages your installation. Learn More

---

Chapter 4: The New Threats

"Let me assert my firm belief that the only thing we have to fear, is fear itself." -
FDR

While most "computer geeks" can beat a dead horse running virus scans on your machine, many/most are not aware of The New Threats. These are threats I've identified as the latest and greatest, and by definition impervious to virus scanners. Identifying them and exposing them is the first step in stopping them.

New Threat #1: Corporate Spyware/Adware/Bloatware

Your typical neighborhood computer guy doesn't realize many of the threats today are 100% legal. That's right, legal. They're created and injected into your machine by companies. These are evil companies consisting of evil managers, evil lawyers, evil secretaries, evil file cabinets, evil water coolers, evil conference tables, and evil fish tanks, but companies nonetheless.

These threats are either placed there without your knowledge (and will leave the machine if you confront them), or they pose as a cleaner/scanner, convincing you that you need them, or they simply slip in underneath something you needed to install.

Bloatware

When you buy a brand new PC today, it is artificially hindered. It comes out of the factory infected with **bloatware**, which is legal software that:

- Cannot help you in any substantive way, but it is a manufacturer's desperate attempt to differentiate itself
- Slows you down
- Nags you throughout the day
- Begs you daily to register your product
- Advertises to you
- Scares you with contrived security alerts
- or...
- Calls home to
  - Download more unsolicited garbage
  - Report what you're doing with your computer

People sometimes call me and say, "I want to get an estimate on fixing my old computer. If it's too high, I'll go buy a new one." To that I always respond, "You can buy a new computer, but at that point, you'll *definitely* need to hire me to scrub it!" Imagine buying garbage bags that came ¾ full, or buying a perfectly good new house, whose windows were smashed! You'd then have to pay for someone to repair it before you could use it.

Apple is the only major manufacturer that has (so far) kept their products nice and clean out of the box. So, if you're in the market for a Windows machine, every major manufacturer includes bloatware (some more than others). You can have it cleaned off for you, or you can have a desktop custom-built instead.

Daemons

Some of these threats come in the form of **daemons**, tiny evil programs that "haunt" your computer, usually legally and without your knowledge.

Did you know?

Let's talk about that wonderful little driver CD that comes with HP printers. You know, that one they say is required for functionality?

If you're not careful, here's some of the software that many printer manufacturers try to sneak into your machine:[54]

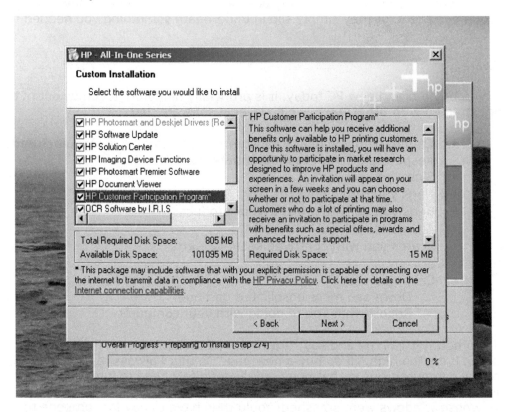

- Customer Participation Program (a.k.a. Product Improvement Study): You probably didn't know this, but you've been a subject of this study since the day you bought your printer! They monitor *who knows what*, presumably something to do with your printing behavior, and report back to the factory.

- Updaters: Guess what! This one calls home and requests that updates be injected into your computer throughout the day. This allegedly helps your printer perform better, blah blah blah. *Who do you think you are? You think you own this printer?*
- Ink Alerts: Another excellent example is ink alert software. These programs pop up and try to sell you ink. End of story.

If you learn nothing else from this book, remember these printer driver CDs inject a whole smörgåsbord of spyware into your PC.

Nagware/Adware

This is simply software that nags you constantly and either advertises or monitors you. Here are some examples:

- ASPCA's We-Care program. It makes money off of you and sends you endless popups. I'm sure 4 or 5 people around the world installed it willingly, but several times a month I remove it for people who have no idea how it got onto their machines.[43]
- Real Message Center: This product stows away underneath copies of RealPlayer, a product I haven't needed since 1999.[42]

Fake Cleaners

In the post-Microsoft world, bad guys realized they don't have to write viruses anymore. They can get into people's machines much more easily by claiming they're there to help. Imagine a bank robber entering a bank and saying "What's up guys, I'm the plumber!" and then proceeding to rob with impunity. Fake cleaners are like snake oil, promising to SPEED UP YOUR PC by cleaning the nonexistent monsters under your bed, such as cookies, outdated drivers, or registry errors. Once you install a fake cleaner, they instead slow your machine down dramatically, run fake scans throughout the day, declare outrageous statistics, then bully you for money.

The tragedy here is that they take advantage of those who are in desperate need of help. They prey on the fearful, make them feel as though they're here to help.

Technically, these are legal, because you agreed to the installation. Ironically, oftentimes these companies even pay the nominal "textbook & bumper sticker" fee to become Microsoft certified, so you feel comfortable as they worsen your machine and charge you money for the privilege. They walk right through any anti-virus scanners as if they're saying, *"These aren't the Jedi you're looking for."*

Toolbars

Oh boy. I could write a whole book about these. Listen up:

Toolbars are software programs that sneak in underneath other programs. They legally latch on to your web browser, cause it to crash, slow you down, change your homepage to their own site, redirect your Web searches, and sell them to somebody. Nobody on Earth wants or needs a toolbar.

A toolbar-infested PC whose toolbars have actually become jealous of each other.

Remember, toolbars are spyware/adware and corrupt your browser, but they're 100% legal. As the Huffington Post put it, "it's a dirty secret that the anti-virus programs you've paid good money for are not going to protect you."[46]

The most common ways to become infected with a toolbar:
- Perhaps you searched online and downloaded Firefox from an impostor site
- You installed that HP driver CD, which sometimes installs Bing Bar
- You let your kids or grandkids download "free games" online
- Your aunt's cousin's friend's pastor's dog's goldfish's cousin's nephew came over and installed a fake cleaning program that exploded toolbars all over your machine
- While looking for a legitimate map site, you were infected with a map toolbar

Examples of Toolbars

Here are some examples of wonderful legal companies who would love to "assist" you in your searches:
- Ask.com
- Mysearchdial
- Mywebsearch
- Babylon
- Bing Bar
- AOL Toolbar
- Coupon Bar
- TelevisionFanatic
- Yahoo! Toolbar
- Astromenda
- Snap.do
- Search Here
- Trovi
- Delta Toolbar
- Safesearch (so ironic)
- Even anti-virus providers are making toolbars now!

Vigilance

In conclusion, be careful not to download any programs from the Internet, unless you're absolutely certain you're on the website of the official provider. Even if you're at the original provider's page (especially with printer and weather alert software), make certain that provider isn't trying to "bundle" other software with the program.

New Threat #2: Update Attacks

Imagine buying a nice new car. Then, imagine the salesman hunting you down for the next ten years, throwing clumps of duct tape at your windshield while you're trying to drive, or smashing into your garage to modify your engine while you sleep. Some weeks, he relocates your steering wheel or gas pedal to suit his whims. Unfortunately, this is the state of the software industry.

Many software products arrive in your hands rough and unfinished, and are in constant contact with the publisher once you own them. When a new version is released, they persistently alert you to this fact, and make it your responsibility to add this constant stream of bubble gum and duct tape to the product. Some programs nag you as soon as you launch them, and others nag you throughout the day even if you don't use them. The annoyance compounds when you have several update attackers all clamoring at the same time! (Mac and Linux have a unified updater which at least keeps it organized.)

Update attacks mean well, promising to improve or fortify a product, but here are some of the challenges they pose:

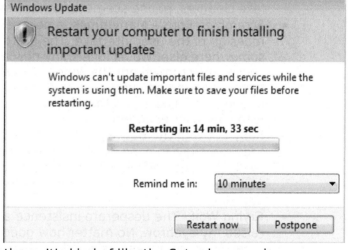

- Massive annoyance – Windows Update is so determined to install an update that it will sidetrack your work and badger you to restart. Many can take 45, 60, or more minutes to install.
- Collateral damage – For whatever reason, update attacks sometimes fix one component and break a few others. It's kind of like the Saturday morning cartoons where they were in a sinking ship. They'd plug one hole and two more jets of water would pop up!
- Violation of your choice – It's usually unclear how to decline the update attacks you don't want, the ones that are known to damage your machine, or protect yourself from them altogether. In the best case, you have to search through a product's menu system and ask it politely to leave. In the worst case, a computer technician has to hunt down the update engine and disable it.
- Violation of ownership - They're the result of an industry that never bothers to complete a project, and characteristically looks down on its users. This isn't just a case of next year's model being worse: Publishers release what's essentially a prototype and figure they can always touch it up later *when it's*

in your house.

- Slow You Down – While devices have been getting faster, newer software becomes more greedy and bloated at a faster pace. How much slower is your smartphone or computer after each update attack?
- Covert Ops – Did you notice your computer become a bit slower after you installed a certain program? The update attackers it introduced are using your computer's horsepower to call home, report *who knows what* to them, and to nag you. You may think you have a virus, but really they're just calling home behind your back.
- Untested – These can and do create instabilities in your system. When I encounter a PC whose copy of Windows is damaged, it's often due to a sour update. Alarmingly, many large businesses don't bother testing updates before deploying them across thousands of employees' machines. The organization grinds to a halt until they can patch up the patches.
- Useless – Imagine having a white picket fence around your house. You faithfully patch the fence to ensure thieves don't enter. Then they arrive in helicopters! No amount of updates to your picket fence can protect you from fake cleaners, phone scams, or other New Threats.
- Scrambled Eggs – Many times, a new version will come with a complete redesign of the user interface: The buttons that used to be here are now somewhere else. We all love shiny new things, but recently we've seen consistency thrown out the window. How many of you enjoy completely re-learning a product every year? (Perhaps the industry could offer two styles of update attacks – one that deals with security and another one that deals with your user experience.)
- Baby out with the Bathwater – Many update attacks add tons of features, then remove the good features that people actually wanted.
- Faulty Airbags – With each new version come billions of useless safety features that serve to further impede the user. This is true even for Firefox and Macs!
- Crying Wolf - The desperate insistence and urgency of update attacks has raised my eyebrow. No matter how good a thing is, if it is presented in such a pushy way, it makes us wonder a bit.
- Questionable Quality – What kind of product needs daily modification? Seems to me something that's either sloppily made or excessively complex.
- Aligning the Stars - Some 1990s business software depends on several building blocks to work in tandem. You then have to make sure all of the stars are perfectly aligned, otherwise it'll crash. Internet Explorer has to be version 7, BusinessProgram1991 has to be version 6, Java has to be version 4350345.6, and Windows has to have Service Pack 2 installed. It's an endless rat race.
- Fake Updaters – If you have kids who watch pirated television shows online, chances are they've been hit with a Fake Updater. These popups claim that your video player is out of date. *Come on, do the right thing and update. Updates are good.* Click on them and they roast your computer.

Examples of Update Attacks

- Logitech Updater - So you bought a webcam from Logitech, and were convinced that the camera wouldn't work without the driver CD. Now, every five seconds a popup from Logitech downloads and installs new software for a camera that already worked fine before you put the CD in.
- HP Update – Do you really need a program that calls home constantly to download newer printer drivers, then nags you relentlessly to update the updates? *What, did you think this was your computer?*
- Adobe Reader – Adobe Reader allows you to read PDF documents (a great industrial standard). The whole world needs to read PDFs, but how many of us need the stowaways that come with each version?
- Java – The idea behind Java was this: A computer programmer could create a program for Java and then Java would enable the program to work on any platform. So, I could design a game for Java, and my game would then run on any Windows, Mac, or Mint machine that had Java installed. Unfortunately the result was a disaster: Only 7 or 8 websites on Earth require you to have Java installed, but many people have it installed nonetheless. Having it installed exposes you to two hazards:
  - First and foremost, customers infected with Java are subject to constant, desperate, relentless update attack notifications. This is compounded by the fact that it invokes UAC, so every five minutes, a machine burdened with Java is HALTED, the screen turned grey, a BOING noise blasts through your speakers, and you're presented with a YES or NO choice for Java Updater.
  - Second is the fact that Java opens up a huge back door for Java-powered viruses to attack at any time. Even the U.S. Government realizes Java has no future and recommends disabling it.[62]
- Adobe Flash - Here's another rat's nest: Flash, like Java, was conceived as a way for programmers to make software and "rich web technologies" (think online videos, or car customizer sites) available to people on all platforms. In fact, it was the *enabling technology* that allowed YouTube to become so successful. Eventually a majority of websites on Earth came to employ the ultra-proprietary Flash technology. Adobe realizes this, and they know you can't live without them. (What are you going to do, not use the Internet?) By 2010, every computer on said planet that had Flash installed would receive an update attack once every few minutes. The reasons for this desperation were: First, flaws are discovered in Flash all the time, and second, when you appease one of these update attacks, Adobe "suggests" stowaway products, such as the McAfee Security Scan Plus (relentlessly bullies you into buying their products). Is this a violation of privacy and trust? I'll let you decide. Luckily, change is on the way. There is a new open standard that will soon replace Flash, called **HTML5**. HTML5 is a universal standard, owned by all of humanity, that is safer, less needing of maintenance, and doesn't invite any friends to come over and play.

- Windows Update – Aside from the constant malware, Windows users also suffer with Windows Update attacks. These emanate from Microsoft HQ over in Redmond, WA, in an attempt to fill up the zillions of security holes they constantly discover. While doing something important, a window pops up, telling you to restart, either now or later, now or later, now or later... until you actually give in. This results in an hour of your day wasted as your computer gives itself surgery. "Don't unplug me! I'm doing something!" Not only does this violate your ownership, but one of these can roast the computer. Very, very often people call me thinking their hard drive is dead, when in reality their copy of Windows was completely roasted after an update. Again, these updates cannot protect you against the other New Threats.

Awareness Is Half the Battle

Look, we all like new toys, cars, and clothes. We all crave a sense of continual improvement and progress. Some of us have even discovered the joy of sculpting a statue or a book. However, computer guys who change things for change's sake are poisoning the well. Some new products contain improvements, but are often accompanied by fatal flaws, and we customers feel compelled to accept this. All too often, companies brag about how quickly their new versions are being adopted: Would they willingly choose your product if given an alternative? *Oh look, Supreme Leader won the election for the 50th year in a row!*

How many of you have had computers completely destroyed after a major update? How many of you have gotten away unscathed from an update attack that hit your smartphone? Anyone? Remember, people once believed pesticides and margarine were improvements, too.

I'm not advocating that you stop doing update attacks – but I'm here to raise awareness, and to advocate for the consumer's right to say no. For example, newer PCs and mobile devices don't allow the consumer to turn off update attacks. **You should have the right to deny update attacks, especially considering how destructive they can be.** Thanks to anti-virus and firewalls, viruses no longer spread from machine to machine, so you're not hurting your neighbors.

If you really want to do updates, you or your technician can tell the nagging updaters to calm down, and then do them at YOUR leisure, not when the publisher attacks. That way, you can actually get your work done once in a while.

Coda: A New Level of Desperation

Are you ready for the concepts of *ownership and freedom* be obsoleted? In 2016, Microsoft auto-inserted a program codenamed GWX (I dubbed it "The Windows 10 Intimidator") into almost every Windows 7 and 8 machine in the world. The level of desperation was unprecedented. It became more and more insistent as time went on, and offered no clear way to opt out.

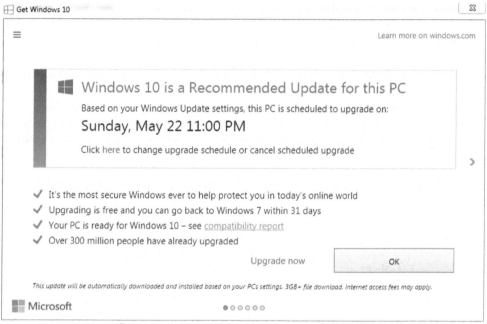

Do you see a "NO" button? Me neither.

In June of that year, one of the trending news feeds on Facebook was the backlash against the Windows 10 Intimidator. It came out that if the user fought against the constant nagging, Microsoft **would then simply auto-install Windows 10!**

I've heard stories of engraving machines, live TV weather report computers, and others crucial computers being interrupted with messages and being forced to reboot, because they felt like changing your machine, and they can do it whenever they want. Facebook user Benjamin Ferrante put it this way:

It is a different world than it was just a decade ago. If a company tried these tactics back then nobody would buy their products. But consumers have been slowly acclimated to this practice. The real issues of security threats is used to help their control over the users.

That same month, a customer successfully sued Microsoft for its auto-attacking behavior.[35] The Windows 10 Intimidator inserted itself into her computer, and constantly berated her for not "upgrading" to the product that she didn't want. When she finally hit the red X button (which is a universal symbol for CLOSE), the Intimidator took it as a "yes" and auto-inserted Windows 10 into her machine. As is often the case, Windows 10 destroyed her computer's ability to run business software.

Updating to Windows 10 has in some cases:
- Roasted a user's programs,
- Mangled their user data,
- Crippled the speed of the machine,

and in all cases:
- Removed your ability to run certain older software, perhaps including that 1990s program your small business depends on to exist,
- Inserted new things such as the Newspeak-esque "Get to Know Me" function. This anti-feature collects information about what you type and who you know. Is it possible that this is why Microsoft wanted us all to switch so badly?

There's one really interesting new "feature" to Windows 10. Hear it from the horse's mouth:

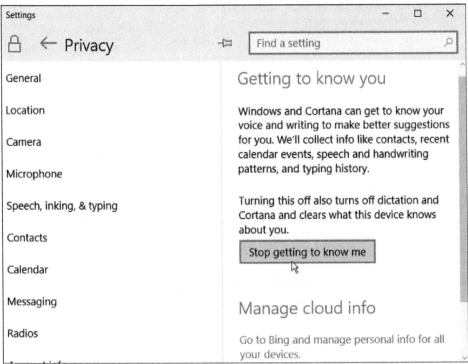

Did you know Microsoft was getting to know you?

Did you know of anyone who actually wanted or needed the Windows 10 update? More people are beginning to sue Microsoft, holding them accountable for their sloppy products after all these decades. Hopefully this will shine a light on the destructive nature of update attacks, and set a precedent that forbids forced auto-attacks. Blogger dedoimedo.com says:

Give the user a feeling that they count, that their desires count. This way, they simply alienate power users, people who do not want to upgrade their boxes, and people who value their freedom.[72]

Sure, the GWX controversy is over, but stupidity still abounds. Remember the analogy about the car salesman? Some new cars are now receiving update attacks "over the air" as you drive... it's happening...

New Threat #3: Hostageware (aka Hoax Viruses)

Hostageware, or Hoax Viruses, are very different from the traditional viruses we grew up with. These babies are BAD. First off, they don't spread from machine to machine: Rather, they come from compromised websites. You can come across one by using Google Image Search, looking at porn, or clicking on a phishing email that impersonates a bank or shipping company. The other point to note is that these guys can cut through a standard Windows machine like a hot knife through butter. Even if a technician can locate them, they even instruct the computer to deny their existence. They are completely unstoppable by normal Internet Security software, and here's what happens next...

First Generation

Your machine is immediately hijacked and you can't run anything. They'll run a fake virus scan, posing as an anti-virus product. They then display a list of every known virus, claiming you have all of them. They'll then present a "Register for full version!" button, and ask you for your credit card number. If you give them this credit card number, you're in trouble. Don't expect your local police to be able to do

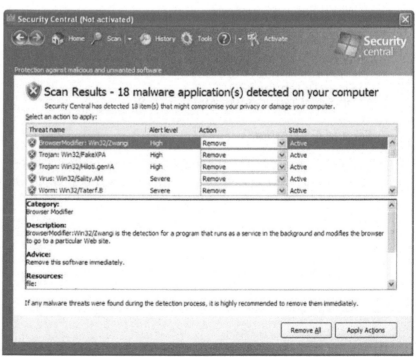

much about these guys, but be sure to call your credit card company and report a scam. Ideally, they'll give you a refund and a new card.

ON TOP of all this, it hides all of your files, making you think you've lost them. THEY ARE still present; just hidden. Even after removing the hostageware and UN-hiding all your files, your User Folder is roasted, so we migrate your documents/photos to a new one.

They usually have pretty shady names, like:

XP Antivirus 2010
Vista Security Pro 2010
Vista Antispyware 2010
Spyware Protect 2009
Antivirus 360
Antivirus XP 2008
Windows Ultra Antivirus
Defense Center
Windows Stability Center
XP Antivirus 2012
Internet Security 2010
Win 7 AntiVirus 2011
Antivirus Security 2013
Win 7 Defender 2013
Security essentials [sic] 2010
Antivirus Clean 2011
Internet Protection
Personal Antivirus
Cloud AV 2012
Win 8 Security System
Security Central
Live Security Platinum
System Care Antivirus
Antivirus Antispyware 2011
SmartDefender PRO
OR SOMETHING SIMILAR.

Second Generation

The second generation of Hoax Virus is very similar to the first generation, except it doesn't leave a roasted User Folder in its wake. Once we remove one of these guys, we don't have to create a fresh user account for you.

Third Generation

These are just hilarious. This hoax harnesses the power of Internet Explorer (digital Swiss cheese) to lock your machine in Kiosk Mode. You're unable to click or touch anything at all, and it presents you with a fake FBI website. They claim you were looking at pornography, and if you don't want your family to find out, you'll mail "The FBI" a money order (to some basement in Africa or Eastern Europe) and they'll magically cancel your jury trial and forgive you.

The Solution

Why do people do this? Because it's incredibly easy to cast a net that reaches thousands of people, and even if 1% of 100,000 people were to fall for one hoax, that's 1,000 people paying $300 each... enough said.

At this point, your Average Computer Guy will do one of the following:
1. Be suckered into the scam, and ERASE YOUR COMPUTER ENTIRELY, destroying all your documents.
2. Admonish you for not running regular virus scans (only you and I know these aren't regular viruses), and then proceed to run some scanners of their own.

A highly knowledgeable technician will know how to remove these guys. My team uses highly advanced software to obtain an honest bird's eye view of the hard drive. We then manually search through all the "usual hiding spots" for these guys and blow 'em to bits. We then make sure all your files are intact, and ensure you have a *proper backup solution in place for the future*.

New Threat #3 ½: Cryptolocker Ransomware

The Nightmare

Oh baby. If the last group was bad, these guys are ruthless. You start out by stumbling upon some infected website, again through web browsing or by clicking on a phishing email.

Here's what happens when you're hit with a **cryptolocker** ransomware:
1. They spend the next bunch of hours scouring your entire computer, **scrambling every document and photo you have**.
2. They then go through any network drives in your office, and attached backup hard drives (some dimwit computer guys recommend you keep your backup drives plugged in perpetually), scrambling everything.
3. They then insert a text document into every folder with crazy instructions on how to get your stuff back. They suggest you go to a seedy back-alley website and pay them via Bitcoins.
4. There are some problems with this:
    ○ Most computer users can't figure out how to do simple things, no less navigate to a seedy website and pay for a hostageware scam!
    ○ The money will inevitably be funneled to actual terrorists, and it's very unlikely they'll actually de-scramble your documents.
    ○ Their preferred method of payment is the untraceable digital currency called **Bitcoin**. While Bitcoin is a method of payment that's morally neutral, disasters like this give Bitcoin an undeserved stigma!

The solution

1. Don't pay them. See why above.
2. Everything on the machine is roasted, and erasing the computer is the only solution, end of story.[63] We're going to pray you have a REAL, PROPER, DISCONNECTED backup in your fire safe, so we can restore your documents to you. (Luckily the forces of good are just starting to figure out how to defeat these. The good news is, most cryptolockers are based on the same handful of platforms.)
3. I've seen plenty of machines that had the usual brands of anti-virus software that were easily hit by these guys. If the consumer was reluctant to switch away from Microsoft computers before this moment, this is usually the tipping point.

Perhaps due to its hazy understanding of the industry, the media has claimed that hospitals, governments, and school districts have been targeted by cryptolockers. In reality, these are booby traps that are set for anyone and everyone. It's usually just some employee searching for Kim Kardashian articles and stumbling into the trap.

Awareness, folks. Stop searching for gossip websites and don't pay anyone.

New Threat #4: Support Scams aka Indian-Style Scams

These scams are all the rage these days, and the world needs to be aware of them.

So far, there are 3 different styles of Support Scams. These are done by evil companies, usually registered in California, with offices in India or Singapore using American VoIP phone numbers (we'll explain VoIP in Chapter 7: The Future).

1. The first type is brought to you by search engine ads, and your desire to speak to someone in the tech support field. If you ever perform a Google/Bing/whatever search for *anything* tech support (e.g. Outlook tech support, Windows tech support, AOL tech support), you'll be met with evil advertisements from evil companies claiming to be able to help you with your issue. (Go ahead, try it out!)

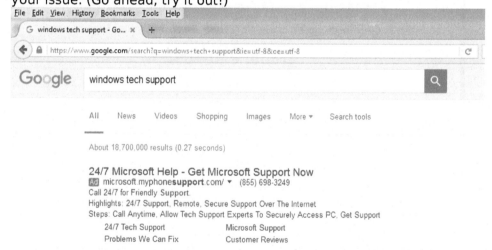

2. The second way is via an unsolicited phonecall. The caller claims they "work for Windows" or "work for Windows Defender", "work for Quickbooks" which are products, not companies. Many will say they're a Microsoft partner and that Microsoft told them you had an issue (untrue). The most brazen will simply claim they're from Microsoft. They'll claim that your computer has

recently downloaded some "malwares and viruses" and will soon "crash down" unless you let them "repair" it.

3. A third style cropped up recently. In this, the scammers hijack a trashy celebrity gossip website, or set up one that's a misspelling of a popular website. like gmaill.com. You arrive at the website and they put a scary paragraph up that makes you think your computer/tablet is infected. Ironically, they're the infection.

WARNING!

SYSTEM MAY HAVE DETECTED VIRUSES ON YOUR COMPUTER

System May Have Found (2) Malicious Viruses: ***Rootkit.Sirefef.Spy*** and ***Trojan.FakeAV-Download***. Your Personal & Financial Information **MAY NOT BE SAFE.**

For Help Removing Viruses, Call Tech Support Online Right Away:

1(855) 970-1892
(TOLL-FREE, High Priority Call Line)

Your IP Address: | Generated on **02-18-2014** | Priority: Urgent

REGARDLESS OF HOW THEY CONTACT YOU, you're on the phone with them, and they'll then scare you with a fake security assessment. Their goal is to convince you that your PC/tablet/smartphone/Mac/Kindle/toaster/stove/toilet has a virus. If it's a PC, they'll:

*   Run a fake utility of their own creation displaying a list of viruses you don't actually have.
*   Run Event Viewer, which is a list of all the most innocuous, harmless non-events your computer keeps track of. Think of it as a journal of sneezing or blinking.

...and then claim you're in trouble. They'll claim you have thousands of trojans, cookies, "hacks", or identity thefts. They'll then offer a one-time price of around

$250-400, or lifetime support for $600-1000, or maybe a monthly fee of $29.99, for a *placebo* that "saves you" from these phantom threats.

Listen up:

Do not believe these people. Their claims, no matter how dramatic, are absolutely baseless. They are trying to scare you into giving them money.

Why do people fall for this? It's because the computer industry has us so trained to fear the buzzwords, such as "viruses", "hacks", and "identity theft".

In a most ironic twist, most of these people have also paid the nominal "textbook & bumper sticker" fee to say they're Microsoft certified technicians! Another example of how my industry curls up on itself like a stack of crooked bricks. Now you see the big picture.

Imagine if I went door to door in your neighborhood, telling people they have bubonic plague, typhoid, leprosy, and polio, then asking for $1000!

Fighting back

The lesson here is that anti-virus software is basically helpless. It usually just protects against primitive viruses, but not Cryptolocker/Ransomware. They certainly can't protect you from fake cleaners (legal) and Support Scams (emotional). They can't protect you from scary paragraphs or phonecalls that cause an emotional reaction of panic! We've got an industry doing updates and scans while the bad guys are walking right in.

Before some marketingbobblehead suggests all websites should get an approval before the public is allowed to see them, we simply cannot rely on reactionary "security databases". Keeping "after-the-fact" lists of virus definitions and good/bad websites is old-school thinking: Many times a day, a new company launches to perform the same scam. Every year, completely new *types* of scams come out. For example there are new phone scams where the caller claims to be the IRS, or your local power company, and claims you owe them money. One guy called me declaring that he was an FBI agent, and threatened me with "a big court battle in Washington D.C." if I didn't mail him $700 in gift cards.

Don't bother calling your local police; they have no jurisdiction over some overseas prankster. The best response is to have some fun with the caller and of course tell all your friends to buy this book!

The only way to truly combat this is to *raise awareness* for:
- the presence of such scams,
- the fact that viruses really don't happen anymore (and these support clowns can't fix them),
- the ways to smell a rat and how to question them (for example, ask them if they know your name, and the answer is of course no).

The computer industry is like a giant Chinese Finger Trap: The more you worry, the more likely you are to pay for fake protection and fake cleaners.

Chapter 5: How it's DONE, Son!

"The definition of insanity is doing the same thing over and over again and expecting different results." - Albert Einstein

Here's how it's done.

Overwhelmed yet? Don't worry! My goal here is that you become informed and thus less intimidated. The rest of the book will teach you the ways to *protect* yourself from this whole industry.

What we'll do is identify and remove these New Threats, as opposed to repeatedly throwing money at a golden calf just to feel better about ourselves.

Here's what Teknosophy-trained technicians do on a typical job:
- Arrest any daemons that haunt your computer.
- Remove any legal programs that were spying on you or implementing paranoia that wastes your time and money.
- Remove any really bad guys, such as rootkits.
- Protect the computer with tools that *actually help* and prevent bad guys from entering in the first place.
- Make sure your documents are *actually backed up* by hand, as opposed to a feel-good auto-backup that might not work if you ever needed it.
- Make sure you're not paying for unnecessary services.
- Prevent your printer from sucking all your money out of your wallet.
- Protect yourself from the most common Update Attacks.
- Make sure your future purchases are safer, more solid, and more cost-effective.
- Make sure your email functions properly and isn't destroyed if your computer dies.

Exorcise those Daemons

We start out by hunting for daemons (evil companies that haunt your machine and slow it down). In order to do that, we launch MSCONFIG, which is a Windows user's best friend. This allows you to see a list of daemons. When you install software, they'll often insert a daemon, because they figure, *Oh well, the software isn't thaaat intrusive.*

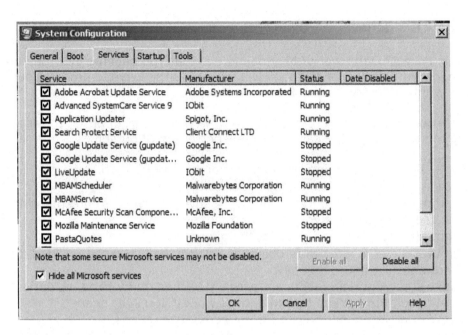

There are two categories we care about: Services and Startup. We'll talk about Services first. You must click "Hide All Microsoft services" so you don't mess with those by accident. Those are crucial to the operation of your machine. After hiding those, what's left are the third party ones that have walked into your machine. You now have the opportunity to disable them.

Next is the Startup tab. (Note that newer machines redirect you to the Task Manager to show you the Startup list.) From here you can disable all Startup items (with exception of Microsoft Security Client if applicable), then you can hit OK and reboot the computer. Lest you say "Wait, I needed one of those items!" understand that we're just arresting the *auto-launching* programs, not removing them. From now on, these programs launch when YOU want, not when THEY want.

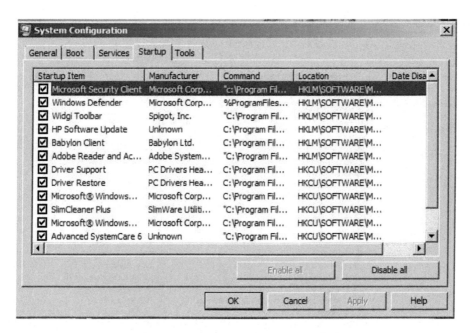

After you reboot, you'll realize two things:

1. your computer is eight hundred trillion times faster and more private
2. your computer for the first time in history is YOURS, as opposed to being an advertising machine for HP, RealPlayer, McAfee, The Weather Channel, and so on.

A small number of programs require their daemon to be running. If you encounter a program that no longer works, simply go to MSCONFIG and reenable that particular company's daemons and reboot.

And Stay Out!

Now that we've prevented all the programs from launching automatically without your knowledge, we're going to completely remove the most damaging ones. For this, we'll go to Control Panel, then *Programs and Features*. This is the most nebulous part of the process, since we have to determine if each of these is dangerous.

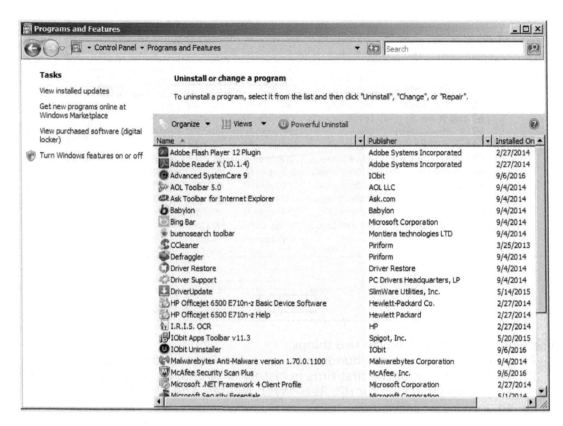

You may have to do some research on each one, but here's what I remove:
- Anything that says Toolbar is an unwanted piece of spyware that's 100% legal.
- Anything that says Weather is probably filth. They claim to alert you to weather updates, all the while inviting in any stowaways that pay them.
- Internet Security products slow a machine down, sometimes by 90%, and implement paranoia around the machine. Of course, they don't know how to protect against the New Threats.
  - Remember, Microsoft includes free anti-virus software that's beautifully unobtrusive and free. In XP, Vista, and 7, it's known as Security Essentials, a free download. In 8 and 10, it's called Windows Defender, and built-in to the product.
  - If you insist on an Internet Security product, many ISPs will give you a free copy upon request. My friends in enterprise-level IT recommend Kaspersky. Expect your computer to work at a snail's pace from then on.
- Anything that says Updater is probably useless filth. We already discussed the reasons earlier. Again, if you want to update periodically, you may do so yourself. Removing the update attacker doesn't prevent manual updates.
- Any weird misspelled things, such as SsaVvinggS CooUPon. These are the shadiest kind of toolbars, usually written by completely unidentified sources,

meant to spy and advertise.
- Anything that says Customer Participation or Survey. Those are legal spyware that monitor your behavior and report it somewhere. Bet you didn't know they were doing that, now did you?
- Driver updater/cleaners/optimizers. While real drivers are necessary, you should never obtain drivers from anyone besides the manufacturer. Anything claiming to optimize or update drivers is just there to beg you for money and slow you down.
- Any fake optimizers or registry cleaners. Basically, anything promising to clean. They're simply wasting your time removing irrelevant things or asking for money.

Keep:
- Any programs that you know you need, obviously.
- Anything that says Visual Basic, C++, XML, SQL, or Framework. Those files support programs you have.
- Anything that says Basic Device Software, such as your legitimate printer driver.
- Legitimate drivers, such as Realtek sound/ethernet, Atheros WiFi, and so on.
- *Any programs you're unsure of,* until you do some research as to what they are.
- Don't worry if you didn't get everything; you've put a significant dent in the malicious software.

Removal of Update Attackers

At this point, we can remove update attackers. These are products that lurk in the background and call home every week, day, hour, or minute looking for newer and more confusing software products to inject into your computer, oftentimes without your consent.

We may have removed some of these while disabling daemons in MSCONFIG. However, some of them require that you ask them politely on their own terms to leave:

Java
- Go into Control Panel and look for a Java icon. Double-click on it and look for an Updater tab. Once there, uncheck the "check for updates" box. At that point, a massive warning symbol will appear, and it will try to bargain with you to check less often. Deny them that pleasure and hit ok.

Windows Update
- In versions PRIOR to Windows 10, it was relatively easy to disable Windows Update. You simply went to Control Panel, Windows Update, Change Settings, and said Never or No to every question.

- If any balloons come up trying to scare you into reenabling, you can ignore Action Center or disable it in "Turn System Icons On or Off".
- In Windows 10, however, consumers aren't allowed to fully disable Windows Update attacks! There are some shortcuts and technical tricks to stop it, but are we as a society going to let this happen?

Adobe Flash

- If you want to stop this boy from crying wolf, Go to Control Panel (or in Mac: System Preferences), then Adobe Flash. There you'll be able to tell it to never nag you again.
  - Unfortunately, the nagging doesn't stop there. Web browsers are becoming increasingly annoying in their fervor to make sure your Flash and other add-ons are updated. If your add-ons are more than five minutes old, web browsers are going to nag you about them. I simply ignore them and update at my own convenience, not whenever they beg me to.

Resurface the computer with proper tools

If our computers use safer products in the first place, we'll end up with a lot less problems.

Now we'll install some programs that ACTUALLY PREVENT security issues from happening, such as a safer browser or safer email. I carry with me an arsenal of my most frequently used tools to make people's machines safer once and for all. Here's what I usually install:

Adobe Reader

As slap-happy as Adobe is, we need their Reader product to read PDFs. (The PDF is a decent universal standard they created to ensure people on any brand/type of computer can send each other documents and they'll appear perfectly.)

If you have Adobe Reader DC, it's the 2015 version that comes with an unstoppable update attacker, and it's jam-packed with advertisements for their cloud services. If you have DC, you can replace it with Reader XI, then continue to the next step.

If you have an older Reader, such as 9, X, or XI, you have the option to decline update notifications. Launch the program, then go to Edit>Preferences>Updater and tell it never to check for updates. You may need to reboot for it to actually stop nagging.

Note that Mac, Mint, and Windows 10 users don't have to bother installing Adobe Reader – these OSes come equipped to read PDFs natively.

Microsoft Security Essentials

MSE is an absolutely free anti-virus product. Think of it as your consolation prize for having to use Microsoft products. Unlike all of these new paranoid Anti-virus/Internet Security products, it does NOT:

- Nag you constantly
- Slow your machine down by 90%
- Explode during removal
- Cost you $70-100 a year

People call me and ask me how often they need to do scans, what they need to look out for, etc. If its interface asks you to click Update or Scan, go ahead. *Otherwise, you don't have to worry about it. MSE does its thing and it leaves you alone.* Remember, viruses aren't common anymore anyway, and no anti-virus product can protect you against The New Threats, so I don't bother scheduling scans anymore.

The legitimate version is ONLY available at Microsoft's official site, for users of Windows XP, Vista, and 7. For Windows 8 and 10, it is built-in and it is now known as Windows Defender, so just make sure it's enabled.

AdwCleaner

For those of us who miss the days where we could just run a scan and make bad things go away, AdwCleaner is the only other scanner I believe is worthwhile. It is one of the few scanners with the audacity to hunt for those evil, *legal* pieces of spyware such as toolbars and search hijackers, protecting itself by calling them "Potentially Unwanted Programs".

It's even good at removing those super shady ones, such as Astromenda and Snap.do. It'll even weed out infected desktop shortcuts – icons that claim to summon your web browser but actually redirect it to a hijacker website, bypassing your homepage preference.

I usually run it for the customer once every 6 or 12 months, but if someone's itching for a feel-good scan, I let them use AdwCleaner to their heart's content.

ClassicShell

From 1995-2015, when a Windows user pressed the Start Button, the Start Menu appeared. It allowed you to select a program, change a preference, or shut down the computer. After the Windows 8 Plague was unleashed on humanity, that expectation of familiarity was shattered by that thing I've termed Evil Colored Square Mode. ECSM replaced the Start Button with a full-screen gallery of flying squares competing for your attention, inside a completely separate universe, with different rules, different physics, and different behaviors.

Windows 8

Luckily, an entire sub-industry of companies popped up to create patches that replaced ECSM with a replica Start Menu. My favorite of these solutions is ClassicShell, which Windows 8 and 10 users can find at classicshell.net. When installing, I turn off the update attacker.

Mozilla Firefox

Contrary to my customers' insistence, this web browser is not affiliated with Mazola Corn Oil. Like Internet Explorer and Chrome, this is a **web browser** – a software program that allows you to visit websites and read their content. It's a bit naggy at times, but I can tell it to calm down.

Firefox is my preferred browser for many reasons:
- It's not Internet Explorer
- It's open source
- It's made by volunteers and held by a nonprofit
- It's not Internet Explorer

If you dare try and set Firefox as your default browser, Windows 10 will protest. It will then start promoting its own "all new" Edge browser and beg you to give it a chance:

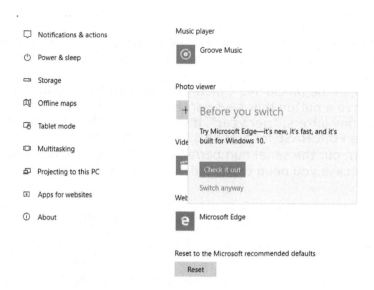

TDSSKiller

As you learned earlier, rootkits are viruses that hide in the basement of your computer. If I work on a computer that looks especially filthy, I'll run Kaspersky's TDSSKiller on it just to be sure there are no rootkits. It's a phenomenal product.

LibreOffice

Back in 2001, a company called Sun Microsystems (familiar to you stock market enthusiasts) played a prank on Microsoft. What they effectively said is, "Hey, you know that thing they're charging $150 for? Why don't we make our own and give it away for free?" So, they did. The product was originally called StarOffice, then OpenOffice, and now **LibreOffice**. Essentially it's a clone of Microsoft's Office (it resembles Office 2003, yes, prior to the mental breakdown known as Office 2007).

LibreOffice costs a whopping $0. This comes in hilarious contrast to Microsoft's new plan where they're trying to rent you the product they used to sell. (What's next, a $10 hammer that you can rent for $9 per year?)

LibreOffice is saving you millions of tax dollars, too! Enlightened government offices in Brazil, France, Ireland, Italy, Germany, Taiwan, Greece, Spain, and Florida have switched.[76]

If you are one of those folks who are:
- petrified by even the slightest aesthetic change
- a Wall Street power-luncher who actually uses the advanced features of Microsoft Office

then you can certainly purchase Microsoft Office online:

- Avoid the Russian-style pirate sites that sell MS Office for a too-good-to-be-true price such as $30. They're 100% fake. Mozy on over to the real website, www.office.com .
- However, *even on the official MS Office website*, you have to watch your step. They'll have a button that says something like "Buy for $99" and underneath in tiny letters, "per year". If you look closely, you can do an actual one-time PURCHASE for around $130 permanently.
- Be SURE to print out the serial number/activation code they give you. Keep that forever, in case you need to rebuild or replace your computer. It's yours!

The rest of us will be over here, grabbing a free copy of LibreOffice. Things to know:

- Don't do an Internet search for "LibreOffice" and get sucked in by an impostor.
  - Libreoffice.org is the only safe source to download and donate.
- By default, LibreOffice saves its documents in its own obscure format. Much like the Esperanto language, the ODT standard was painstakingly designed to be pure/logical/universal, and nobody paid any attention to it.
  - If you care about sharing your documents/spreadsheets with your school/work/friends, you or your technican must flip a few switches first. After installing, go to "Options>Load/Save>General" and tell LibreOffice to save your documents/spreadsheets/presentations as the de facto standard of Office 97, so you can share your creations with others.

Mozilla Thunderbird

Thunderbird is a **mail client** program, in other words an email viewing tool. It is NOT a new email service; rather, it is a tool that allows you to connect to almost any email service, like Gmail or Hotmail.

Thunderbird resembles the familiar Microsoft Outlook or Windows Live Mail interface, but it isn't a welcome mat for email worms and it's not self-destructive[87]. In a few minutes, we'll talk about how I perform a Magical Email Transition for people to make their email work seamlessly.

VLC

Finally, a video/audio program that plays almost everything. You can forget about RealPlayer (one of the pioneers of adware), or the limited Windows Media Player. Just go to videolan.org (NOT videolanD, which is an impostor), and grab VLC. Upon first use, as you'd imagine, I always disable the update attacker.

Proper backup

Let's take a moment to review those myths about backing up your data.

First, let's talk about automated backups. Many computer "experts" recommend automated backups. You leave a hard drive plugged in all day and night, and your computer automatically backs itself up, right? WRONG. Remember the three groups of things in your hard drive: The Operating System, Programs, and your User Folder (aka your stuff).

Many automated backup solutions, such as Western Digital SmartWare, Windows Backup, and even Apple's Time Machine may attempt to back up your OS and Programs, which are virtually impossible to reuse, so they just end up filling up your drive. The only thing that matters is backing up *your user data*, the stuff relevant to you.

YOUR USER DATA	Back up
PROGRAMS	Don't back up
OS	Don't back up

Contents of a typical hard drive

Moreover, automated backup programs might not respect the way you had your data organized. They might plop your stuff into folders based on the day they felt like backing them up, rather than how you had them. Also with this method, if your PC dies, you must purchase another machine of the same platform in order to restore your stuff.

Finally, lest you think leaving a backup drive plugged in constantly is a good idea, remember this:
- A hard drive that's always running means constant wear and tear.
- If you have a fire or flood in your computer room, you lose everything.
- If you're hit with a ransomware/cryptolocker, it'll probably scramble *all* of your data on *anything* connected to your PC, including that backup drive.

Automated backups are neither human-verifiable nor human-readable. They're akin to buying a smoke alarm that looks really spiffy, but doesn't beep during a fire.

Recall that other myth: Many computer "wizards" believe that having lots of user data on your computer slows it down. **That's absolutely false.** That's just as silly as saying "Having too many books in your living room slows your car down!" These guys recommend customers *move* their data onto an external hard drive. *What's wrong with that?* Recall that ANY hard drive can die at any time, often without warning. So, whether internal or external, having your data in ONE place is a terrible idea.

You need a backup hard drive that stores a duplicate snapshot of your stuff. (Sure, you could burn dozens of CDs to back up your data, but it'll take you hours and cause much confusion.) Here's how to create a Teknosophy-style Proper Backup, which has none of those shortcomings. *Don't try this at home, kids, unless you possess advanced file management skills.*

- Start out with an empty thumbdrive or external hard drive. Make sure it has enough space on it for your data.
  - If it's new, delete any preloaded factory garbage first.
  - If you already own one, make sure there's nothing stored exclusively on it that's not also in your computer.
- Create a folder on the external drive with today's date, for example "1 Jun 2015 Backup of my Upstairs Desktop". Open up that new folder. Push the window aside for now.
- Next, open up your User/Home Folder. It'll show you all the categories of stuff you have on your machine, such as your Documents, Photos, Music, Downloads etc.
- Drag each of those folders to the "today's date" folder you created, then wait for them to copy over.
- *Voila,* a proper backup snapshot of only the data relevant to you, which is 100% human readable and verifiable. Keep that drive disconnected and in a fire safe until your next backup.
  - After copying, be sure to Safely Remove/Eject the drive and keep it in your fire safe or a relative's fire safe until you're ready to perform your next periodic backup.

Alternatively, you can find a synchronization program such as Free File Sync. Syncing is better than an automated backup because it performs a simple one-way synchronization from your computer onto your backup drive, without any cryptic databases.

Note that I use this process for residential users. Many small businesses rely on a 1990s-era program that stores information in a database fashion. In those cases, you must ask the computer politely to spit out a backup of the database onto your backup drive.

Cloud Backup

As you know, I recommend periodic local Proper USB backups, but you might want a constant backup service looking out for you. If you're comfortable doing so, you can sign up for an online **cloud backup** service.

An online cloud backup service is a one-lane one-way street that backs up your machine automatically throughout the day. This is great for people who make constant additions and changes to their user data.

**One-Way One-Computer
Online Backup Service**

Backup Service

Examples of such services are Carbonite, Mozy, Crashplan, or my favorite, iDrive. They charge a yearly rate, and back up your machine for you throughout the day. (Note that the tech community considers MyPCBackup and its cousin Zipcloud to be unsavory:[55] They sneak into your machine underneath other things you download, they may not hold your data securely, and constantly ask for more money.[68])

In Case of Rain

If you're going to use online cloud backup, it's a good idea to supplement it with a Proper Backup hard drive, stored in your fire safe. There are plenty of things that can go wrong.

Proper Smartphone Backup

We've all heard of automated smartphone backups: The peace of mind that comes with knowing your portable device can fall off Niagara Falls or Montaña de Oro with little consequence. However, most people just buy a smartphone, take a pile of nice pictures, and just assume they're going to be available someday, somewhere, somehow. Be sure you know what service stores your phone pictures!

If you're super cool, you'll copy them from the picture backup service to your computer. If you're like me and avoid phone backup services altogether, simply copy your photos from your phone to your computer from time to time. Either way, they should be included in your Proper Backup.

Photo Management Mafia

Useless Helper Overlays

I'm in favor of basic conceptual training and basic usability training. For example, knowing how email works, knowing how to Minimize/Maximize/Restore a window, or the difference between copying and moving. (Copy creates a duplicate of the file in the destination folder, whereas move simply moves it into the destination.)

However, the industry feels it can just change its products capriciously and alienate people further.

Here's how the **helper overlay** cycle works:
1. Customer is intimidated by a computer because the computer industry changes things by the minute.
2. Rather than simplifying the process, the industry creates what I call a **helper overlay**, a more complex "shortcut" way to use the machine, and superimposes that interface on top of the standard interface.
3. The user becomes confused, and they lose track of their data.

There are myriad examples of this, from "preview" windows that interrupt when you're trying to download an email attachment, to "favorite" icons when you're trying to see your email folders, and so on.

I understand the urgent need to bring order to this chaotic industry, but adding layers of complexity don't make things simpler. Rather than simply teaching you how ride a bike, the industry puts rockets on the back of it, slaps an "EASY" sticker on it, and thinks they've helped you. Then they wonder why people aren't comfortable.

Such is the case with photo management. People *think* they need a photo management program in order to even *have* photos on their computers, which is untrue. You can import and store photos on any kind of computer made in the past 15 years. You plug in your camera, it imports them to your Pictures folder, and from there you can create subfolders and organize your stuff. Photo Management software can ONLY serve to cause disasters.

Examples of useless photo managers

- Google Picasa
  - More confusing than *Alice in Wonderland*
  - Scans your entire computer for any images, resulting in thousands of tiny useless icons
  - Known to delete or duplicate photos at random, to our chagrin
- Apple Photos née iPhoto
  - Locks all of your photos in one ball called a Photo Library and can create duplicates of everything at random
- Kodak EasyShare
  - Includes a daemon that slows down a Windows computer massively
  - Causes constant Blue Screens of Death
  - Hides your photos from you outside of your home folder, so they aren't backed up
  - Luckily this ~~abomination~~ nice product is no longer offered.

My whole problem with photo managers is this: Instead of holding your photos in your folders where you can organize and name them, most photo managers needlessly keep a database or roster of what THEY named them and where THEY are holding them. This roster can corrupt itself fairly easily, leaving you with one single huge pile of unnamed photos. Of course, nobody learns this until it's too late and their roster is corrupted.

Again, it's simpler to use your built-in photo importer, such as Windows Scanners and Cameras or Apple Image Capture, or just drag and drop the photos from your memory card directly. You are then able to name and organize YOUR OWN PHOTOS YOURSELF in a way that doesn't involve self-destructive rosters. If you need to edit a photo, find a photo editor that doesn't commandeer your entire collection.

Stop making all that racket!

Inkjet printers are another example of a segment that used to be wonderful and now apparently exists only to milk the customer. In 1995, my family used a Hewlett-Packard Deskjet 540. It was well-made, reliable, and actually printed whenever we pressed print! Surely you've noticed how inkjet printers since then have become less predictable, less reliable, less carefully designed, and less efficient with ink... but hey, at least you can walk up to your HP inkjet and browse Facebook on its fancy color screen! *Everyone's going to want that feature!*

Many printers now allow you to buy separate cartridges instead of one containing all the colors, but cartridges for a consumer inkjet printer can easily retail for $50, either per set or per color. Most of them only last 1-3 months!

An average cartridge holds 5mL of ink. Let's say it costs $30. That means for every liter, we're paying $6,000 (about $15,800 per gallon). And you thought gas prices were high!

For most inkjet owners, there comes a time when you'll put in brand new cartridges and still nothing will come out on the page. That's because the **print head** (the part that writes onto the paper) is clogged. The print head used to be a part of the cartridge, so when it clogged it was no big deal. It is now a part of the printer, and it's either permanently integrated or it costs more than the printer itself. If you clean the print head and it doesn't help... landfill here we come!

Leave it to HP to be the overachiever in this segment:
- Some cartridges set themselves to expire after a certain amount of time, whether or not you used it first.[25]
- Some cartridges include computer chips that report to the printer that they're genuine, in an attempt to prevent the use of generic cartridges. Paradoxically, this leads to the printer falsely accusing people who've purchased genuine cartridges.[26]
- Some cartridges will marry themselves to one printer forever, thus preventing you from trading it in to a recycling facility.[24]
- One day, HP Update injected a "sleeper cell" into people's printers. It woke up after 6 months and caused any printers using third-party cartridges to stop printing.[60]

Tons of R&D has been put into the inkjet industry, which might lead us to ask... What went wrong? Was this R&D money put into devising ways to make the experience worse and more expensive? Aside from finding a DeskJet 540 at a thrift store, what's a consumer to do?

Laser is the answer

I'm completely done with ink and use laser printers exclusively. Sound scary to you? The overall cost of a modern laser printer is easily cheaper than inkjets. Black & white laser printer/scanner/copier machines cost around a hundred bucks, and color machines can be had for a bit more. I spend $9 per year for a black toner cartridge. Beats $50/month, doesn't it?

Most laser printers are extremely well-made and are built to last very long in punishing office situations. Lasers use powder cartridges that don't dry up (they're already powder!), and yield thousands of pages.

Be it ink or laser, genuine or third-party, you can save money ordering cartridges online. For example, if you had the Brother LC-61 inkjet printer, Amazon offers a 12-pack of cartridges for $8.55! Just check the customer reviews to make sure the ones you're buying are well-made.[22]

What to Buy the Next Time Around

When people ask me what to buy, I always start out with, "Okay, what do you plan on doing with your machine?" Just kidding. I always start out by ranting about HP. Then, I ask what they plan on doing with their machine.

Remember, out of the three platforms on this page, only Windows machines are subject to viruses/trojans and constant mysterious self-destruction[81]. If you opt for a non-Microsoft machine, it's virtually impossible to have a conventional virus, and super rare to see one of them self-destruct. The only thing you'll have to look out for are those New Threats, like Support Scams and legal fake cleaners.

Windows

If you're a small business, chances are you need weird business programs that were written in 1992, so you should stick with Windows. If you're into the latest 3D games, stick with Windows as well. You can grab a Windows laptop starting at around $300 these days.

Windows comes on most brands of PCs. When I pick a brand, I concentrate on longevity, simplicity of design, and ethics (how much or how little bloatware the factory put in).

My favorite brands are Dell and Lenovo (Lenovo is sort of a spinoff of IBM's PC division), because I see computers from both of those brands that are 15 years old and still running.

Stick with a true laptop or desktop, and avoid the ultra-cheapie stripped down cloudbook devices. You might not be able to run the your software you need, and you usually can't print from them.

Mac

If you have an interest in video editing, or spending money (or just the latter), you'll want a Mac. The Mac Mini is by far the best value, clocking it at around $600, and it has sufficient horsepower for most people. If you have high end needs and budgets, the Mac Pro is the king of the hill. Always avoid the all-in-one iMac: They're twice he price and insanely difficult to repair.

Don't listen to the clowns who say Macs are difficult to use or incompatible with things. Neither is true. Your local mall's Apple retail store is usually staffed with knowledgeable people who can train and support you, and Microsoft offers an identical version of Office for the Mac.

Grab a Mac while you still can: I believe Apple's heading into another dark age of insular proprietary exclusivity and frustrating gimmicks (touchbar, anyone?).

Finally, he discusses Mint!

If you're like 99% of the world and just want to do Internet, email, documents, and be left alone, your prayers have been answered! Mint is a spectacular Operating System that's extremely minimalist and insanely reliable. I don't know about you, but I can't be interrupted with nonsense while I'm doing my work. Get this: You can actually do what you want without your computer crashing on you constantly! It's based on Linux but I never mention that because even average computer guys are terrified of that word. In the form of Mint, though, it's no longer terrifying. (We'll learn about how it came to be in the How It All Works" chapter.)

A typical Mint desktop

Mint blends the extreme stability of Linux with the familiarity of Windows XP/7. It respects the user and works like an appliance – No constant error messages expecting you to solve scary technical issues, no bombardment with popups and "Free AOL" icons.

Note that you can't run QuickBooks or bizarre 1990s business software on Mint. You can only run:
- Firefox
- Thunderbird
- Chrome (and its Netflix extension)
- LibreOffice
- Skype
- Dropbox

- VLC (plays DVDs)
- a few simple games
- and a few other things.

It's ultra minimalist, ultra stable, and ultra safe. Because you can't have traditional viruses, you have no need for Internet Security software that cripples your machine by 90%. I believe it is the perfect solution for the vast majority of people who just want to get online and not live in fear!

Getting One

How do you get a Mint machine? You start out by buying a standard Windows PC, either desktop or laptop. We then erase the hard drive (purifying it of all Microsoft malarkey) and "remodel" it by installing Mint. It's a good idea to do some research to make sure somebody's successfully used Mint with your model of laptop (and printer!).

My shop is the only one in the area that's not afraid to install Mint on PCs, old or new. During a normal service call, we'll ask customers if they've got any virus-ridden machines collecting dust in the closet. We love breathing new life into a secondary PC with Mint!

You can
- Hire us to install Mint on a PC you bought yourself.
- Order one from a retailer like ThinkPenguin.
- Check out Dell and System76; they offer Ubuntu machines which can be converted to Mint.

I believe there is a future for the desktop and laptop PC. I believe the only reason many people went to tablets in the first place was to avoid the complexity and self-destruction[81] of Microsoft products. *Most people still want a large screen, a keyboard, and a mouse. Most people are squinting at their smartphones, trying to use them as computers because their computers are too slow and cluttered to use.* If I could install Mint on every PC in the world, people would actually enjoy using them!

Secondary/travel machines

Chromebook

Chromebook is a cloudbook made by a few manufacturers, running Google's ChromeOS Operating System. Remember, cloudbooks are great for travel, education, or senior citizens. At the moment, the only thing you can do with them is go to websites.

It's virtually impossible to print with one of these babies, since they don't carry any print drivers. If you had to print something, they offer a harebrained scheme where you send your document to *them*, then they send it to your printer at home.

Look for Chromebooks to pop up in more educational outlets as time goes on. Both Chromebooks and Macs are offering their own App stores now, so both of those platforms bring a huge amount of potential once only available on smartphones.

Mobile devices

Let's say you're considering one of these tablets, such as an iPad or an Android tablet. Avoid the cheapie drugstore tablets, since they are horribly slow and break almost immediately after buying them. For my money, the Amazon Fire tablet is a no-brainer. They're half the price of drugstore tablets (start at ~$50) yet have fantastic build quality.

We've all heard about exploding Samsung phones, but here's why I always ignore their kiosks:

- They come with unremovable bloatware/spyware[41]
- The factory can actually send them a remote self-destruct command whenever it feels like it[80]

One of the good things about Apple's mobile devices (iPhone, iPad, etc.) is the ability to print with ease. Simply touch Secret Square Arrow Button (or sometimes it's Secret Arrow Button, not very consistent) and the Apple device looks around you to see if there are any printers compatible with its AirPrint language (most printers are nowadays). There's NO prior setup, NO stupid driver installs! Absolutely fantastic!

Mobile devices are great for travel because they're cheap and you don't really keep much data on them. So if yours falls off a cliff, who cares! My personal travel machines include an Android tablet and a laptop running Mint.

Dockable Smartphones

In the very near future, we'll be able to plop our smartphones on our desks, and plug them into our monitors, keyboards, and mice. It'll then transform itself into a desktop computer so we can work comfortably! This has already been attempted by a guy (you'll soon meet) named Mark Shuttleworth. It's just a matter of time before we see this invention join the chorus of Macs, Mint PCs, and tablets that are eating away at Microsoft's market share.

Chapter 6: How It All Works

"User friendly is expert hostile." - Peter Anderson, computer scientist

Platform Politics

Don't worry, we're not discussing Tories and Whigs. Rather, in this chapter we're going to explain the history of the three major OS platforms. I think it's important that we know a bit about who created the stuff we use today.

"Okay kids, today we're watching a movie." Didn't your high schooler heart leap for joy when you heard those magical words? If you enjoy this chapter, check out the movies *Pirates of Silicon Valley* (1999), *Jobs* (2013), and *The Code: Story of Linux* (2001, available on Youtube). They're super fun and give great insight into the meteoric rise of Jobs, Gates, Torvalds, and friends.

Microsoft Windows

William H. Gates, III dropped out of Harvard to start "Micro-Soft" in 1976 with his poker buddies Paul Allen and Steve Ballmer. (Search for Ballmer on YouTube right now. Isn't he awesome?) Housed in a tiny plaza in Albuquerque, they started out making BASIC-language software for early computers.[3]

In 1981, IBM believed personal computing was a passing fad, but they wanted to have something to bring to the table. They needed a new Operating System for this upcoming product, which they named the... Personal Computer. Here's how legend has it:

IBM called the first programmer, but he was out flying his plane and his wife forgot to take down the message. They then called Bill Gates because they heard he was a smart guy. Not one to turn down an opportunity, he claimed he had just the product for them. The answer-less Gates hung up the phone, started sweating, and went out for a walk in the rain. On that walk, he stumbled upon Seattle Computer Products, which was eager to show off its new invention called DOS. He pulled out his checkbook and bought the company on the spot.

Bill Gates & Steve Ballmer[38]

While that sounded cool, here are the facts:

IBM first consulted Bill Gates, who referred them to a company originally known as (get this!) Intergalactic Digital Research. IBM did indeed meet with IDR (owned by

Gary Kildall, the programmer with the plane), but Kildall's Operating System wasn't yet modern enough for their needs. Gates then searched for company that made software for very similar machines, and he enlisted their help.

The company was Seattle Computer Products, and for around $100,000 Gates bought the *unlimited* rights to their DOS product. Of note is that he *didn't transfer the rights to IBM*, because he foresaw the day when *other* hardware makers (the first one being Compaq) would want to license DOS from him. He charged IBM a license fee for every single PC they sold (and to this day charges manufacturers in the same manner).[2]

Once Kildall saw how similar DOS was to his CP/M OS, he became furious. While he eventually sold out to Novell for a sufficient fortune, he died a young, bitter man. Kildall's friends argue that if he had prevailed, the world wouldn't have to deal with "more than a decade of crashes".[6]

Microsoft went on to launch Windows, Office, the XBOX video game console, and several attempts at a tablet. Bill is spending his retirement as a philanthropist, and Microsoft continues to re-surface Windows with different kinds of duct tape.

Apple Macintosh
Meanwhile, another giant was born, with a decidedly different approach. Steve Wozniak created the Apple computer, and Steve Jobs introduced it to the world from his parents' garage. The goal of Apple was to create products you didn't have to assemble, products that didn't require you to be an engineer.

Like the Lancia car company, their passion for doing things the right way often got them into financial trouble.[7] As the *Jobs* movie depicts, they were criticized for taking the road less traveled, rather than the cheaper option of building on someone else's platform.

Steve Wozniak & Steve Jobs[39]

Their allergy to basing their products on conventional platforms (such as IBM or Microsoft) proved to be the differentiator that allowed them to soar.

Search YouTube for "Steve Jobs Insult Response"[5]. At a developer's conference, a nerd criticized Steve for not knowing some minute detail of programming trivia. Steve responds by telling the tale of how Apple developed the first home laser printer. It was loaded with their vendors' latest tech, but all the customers really cared about was having that warm piece of real paper with words on it (and no more holes in the sides!).

While the entire computer industry freaks out about specifications, how many gigs, how many megs, how many protocols... Steve Jobs was *not* a computer programmer at all, and his mantra was: "Who cares about the technology; what can it accomplish for you?" Have you ever seen an iPhone ad displaying CPU and RAM specs? Neither have I, but look at all the things it can do reliably.

Linux

Unix Origin

It was the summer of '69, and Ken Thompson of Bell Labs spent a month home alone while his wife brought their new baby to visit relatives. During that month, he created **Unix**[9], originally meant as a small work project. Along with coworker Dennis Ritchie, he laid the groundwork for the future of computing.

Ken Thompson, Dennis Ritchie, & Bill Clinton[33]

Unix is an Operating System that runs on servers. (Servers, née mainframes, are heavy-duty air-conditioned computers used by organizations to crunch numbers and keep track of huge amounts of information.) Unix ended up being wildly popular among large organizations, with licenses costing around $10,000 a pop. Thanks to some pumpkin-guts legal situation, the University of California at Berkeley ended up giving away its own version of Unix, called Berkeley Software Distribution. Fun fact: Apple's products are now based on BSD!

Scratching an Itch

Fast-forward to 1991, and we find University of Helsinki student Linus Torvalds waiting in line to use the Unix mainframes at school. The story holds that he went home that summer and saved up for a personal computer so he no longer had to wait in line. Eventually, Linus purchased his new computer and set it up in his dorm room. As soon as he starts using this DOS-equipped machine, he decides it's too medieval, so he erases it and creates his own Operating System, a clone of Unix he calls *FreaX*. His buddy gives it the indisputably better name of *Linux*, which is a portmanteau of Linus+Unix.[11]

Linus created Linux to "scratch his own itch", as we say. The story would've stopped there had he not publicized his creation. What he did next was just as brilliant as creating the software.

He released Linux as Open Source, meaning a few things:

- Cost is $0.
- You are free to redistribute the product.
- You have the right to view the *source code*, (think sheet music or blueprints) that went into creating the software.
- You can freely modify the product to meet your needs.
- If you redistribute a modified version of the software, just give credit where credit is due.
- Sounds like the jazz community, doesn't it?

Open source is sometimes called the Free & Open Source Software movement (FOSS). It is self-regulating and donation-based. Other examples of FOSS products include Firefox and LibreOffice. In a world where governmental transparency and nutritional ingredient labels are valued, it is my prediction that eventually more people will demand transparently-designed software as well.

Linus Torvalds[12]

The current crop of commercial products are generally closed-source, like a secret family chili recipe. With these products, we can only speculate on what they're doing to us. Also, if they go out of business, we may not be able to use the products.

In contrast to this, open source/FOSS means the recipe or blueprints are available for all to see, (note that this does NOT imply that your user data is somehow exposed). Open source products are safer because we can see what our computers are being instructed to do, and make sure they're not reporting things behind our backs to somebody. They're also eternal: If the company or volunteers who create it disappear, no problem, we still have the blueprints.

Dental FOSS

What started out as an engineer creating a tool for himself exploded into a worldwide phenomenon because he believed in FOSS. I can almost hear the voices of Kodak retirees insisting license fees and patent wars are the way to go, but this radical form of generosity paid off indirectly:

- Linus eventually became world-famous. Like most programmers who list an open source project on their resumes, he has no problem getting a job.
- In 1999, Red Hat and VA, two companies who based their products on Linux, went public. Both companies gave him token shares of stock out of gratitude. The morning of the IPO, his shares were worth $20 million.[10]
- Linux now runs on countless devices – such as TomToms, Sony TVs, Android phones, and most smart devices!
- As my elementary school principal said, "Many hands make light work!" Anybody can contribute to an open source project, which results in rapid product development.
- He is now an employee of the nonprofit Linux Foundation, which pays him to be smart and work on Linux whenever he wants.

If FOSS products are meant for the world to have for free, how do FOSS companies make money? The answer is simple – They charge you for tech support, if you need it. In a similar way, I'm revealing my "secrets" in this book because I believe you have the right to know what's out there, and I make money assisting people in their transitions to better platforms.

Hold your Horses

As a concept, Linux is simply fantastic. It signifies legendary stability, transparency, freedom from bloat and stagnation, and it is modifiable by anyone interested. The problem? It wasn't friendly.

By 1999, Linux was only used by highly trained server administrators, its interface too complex and unrefined even for yours truly. Many PC manufacturers still snub those trying to use Linux on their hardware, and Linux enthusiasts themselves scoffed at its use by the proletariat.

I tried it again in 2003, but it was still pretty unrefined. Meanwhile, the public continued to suffer with Windows "bluescreens" and viruses. The Antitrust lawsuits against Microsoft raged on, but Linux wasn't yet a viable alternative.

It Came from Outer Space... sort of.

Enter Mark Shuttleworth. Mark is a an eccentric South African "Internet Billionaire" who had just sold a company for $0.9 Billion. (Close but no cigar, poor guy.)

At first he spent his retirement as a space tourist, but one day in 2004, he got bored and set off to solve the world's problems.

He needed a place with enough peace and quiet to think about this, so he went to Antarctica for a while. There, he read through printouts of discussions from some of the world's top programmers, and picked a few to hire.

That year, Mark formed Canonical, Ltd. and named his new product *Ubuntu*. Ubuntu is an ancient pan-African philosophy with some cool interpretations:

Mark Shuttleworth[56]

- "Humanity toward others."
- "You should applaud rather than tear down those in your village who succeed."
- "You can break a straw but you can't break a whole broom."

Mark's mission for Ubuntu: To craft a Linux that was user-friendly. Many had tried; all had failed. I myself brushed it off as yet another noble attempt! I thought, *"Just what we need, another Linux version with a cool logo and an unrefined interface."*

Alas it survived. By 2008, it was easy enough for the average Joe to use.[8] The world finally had a viable alternative to the explosive Windows and the expensive Mac. I began installing it on machines for customers.

A Fork in the Code

The 2011 revision of Ubuntu introduced a bewildering new user interface that nobody on Earth could figure out. Unfortunately they never retracted it. In the ancient system where a software company releases a product to installers in a one-way fashion, such a disaster would cause strife and helplessness. (Cough, Windows

8, cough.) However, in the new FOSS system, individuals are empowered. A group of nerds decided to make a *fork* in the family tree, so they took the Ubuntu OS and cleaned it up, then released it as the Mint OS. Mint is now my choice for an extremely minimalist, extremely consistent OS. It works just like a normal computer, but it's very unobtrusive and stable. The most empowering part about this is, if I experience an issue, I provide feedback to the Mint or Ubuntu teams, and *they actually do something about it!*

Hacking

Originally, the term **hacker** meant an enthusiast who liked to tinker with technology. Hacking, then, meant modifying a product you own so that it meets your needs. It was only later that the term was used to describe digital vandals.

If all of that sounded idealistic and abstract to you, here's something that will hit home: If you discover a flaw or have an issue with a FOSS product, it's repairable and customizable. Remember, rather than the one-way street where calcified products are foisted on you, the FOSS community believes you should have the right to modify something you own. This forgotten concept is going to be crucial in the future.

And that's how all the major platforms came to be!

The Lowdown on Adobe Flash

In the late 90s, the product known as Flash allowed us to do more with the Internet besides simply reading articles. It enabled us to play games, configure a new car to our tastes, and watch videos. Indeed, it was the technology that enabled YouTube to flourish across all platforms of personal computers.

Unfortunately, these issues brought about its demise:
- Every day, tons of flaws are discovered in this product. As such, it seems as though a new version comes out every five minutes... and when one comes out, they make sure you know about it. Adobe claims "Installed on more than 1.3 billion systems, Flash Player is the standard for delivering high-impact, rich Web content." - That's a lot of jostled users.
- If a customer appeases an update attack, they're taken to a website that suggests they install the latest version. Not so fast: Adobe takes this opportunity to "suggest" that you also install software from one of it friends. Logic dictates that Adobe must receive some sort of compensation for granting the stowaway access to such a large audience.
- It's a major RAM hog. It gobbles up your system resources and slows your machine down.
- It's closed source and proprietary. We have NO IDEA what goes on inside the "black box", nor are outsiders allowed to discover and repair flaws.
- As with many things in the computer industry, it was a monopoly, so there

was no motivation for its creators to change it.

It gets weirder: Every day, kids around the world visit "Watch TV Free" pirate sites. Those sites feature Flash Update impostors. Click on one, and malicious software pours into your machine.

If you need to install Adobe Flash, BE SURE TO ONLY DOWNLOAD IT from their official site, www.adobe.com/downloads . If you do a web search for Adobe Flash, you'll likely get an impostor. Unfortunately, even at the official site, you'll have to be sure to avoid the stowaway software they offer when you download it. During the installation process, you'll be able to disable the update attacker if you like.

Hope

Steve Jobs prohibited Flash technology on Apple mobile devices. This perfectionist didn't want to see his products slowing down, crashing, and running full of security holes for no reason. On mobile devices, Mobile Apps have taken the place of many flash-based websites, delivering rich experiences on mobile devices.

Thanks in part to his push, Flash is going away. As of 2017, HTML5 is finally replacing Flash as the preferred method of delivering those rich Web experiences. HTML5 is a world standard that's owned by no one company, doesn't slow down and expose computers, and most importantly, doesn't bludgeon you with update attacks and stowaways.

Surface Tension

Unfortunately, Mac and Linux haven't yet dominated desktop computers. It took an actual paradigm shift to break Microsoft's monopoly! Not until the dawn of tablet computers, such as iPad and Android, did Microsoft's rivals break through. Millions flocked to them, not just for portability, but for the simple and virus-free Internet experience.

Shortly after the introduction of the wildly successful iPad and Android tablets, Microsoft claimed that "Tablets are a passing fad."[4] (It's kind of like when Kodak downplayed their own invention of digital photography, or when Xerox ridiculed its own invention of the computer mouse. Oops.) Before and after that, Microsoft attempted a few tablets of their own, resulting in varying degrees of failure: Tablet PC, Slate, and Surface.

For a video depiction of Microsoft's Surface tablet at work, simply search YouTube for "Windows 8 tablet FAIL" and enjoy. The video shows the tablet crashing at its own debut just like its grandfather, Windows 98!

On its first Black Friday, at one mall, Surface enjoyed a sales record of precisely 0.[13] They're now in their fourth generation and I've only had two customers who bought them... by accident.

How Email Works

Many jokers have no concept of how email works, and as such, are unable to preserve your email messages in the event of a disaster or migration to a new machine. After teaching this particular session in my adult ed classes, I pronounce my students more knowledgeable than any computer repair guy in town.

There are two types of email systems: POP mail and IMAP mail.

POP

Post Office Protocol, or **POP**, is a protocol from 1988[15] that is ancient and rotten. Only a handful of pathetic email providers still utilize this technology, including most local Internet providers, as well as low-end small business web hosting services.

If you're infected with a POP email account, here's what you're suffering through:
- Duplicate emails showing up on your tablet and computer
    - Or sometimes some messages on your computer and other messages land on your tablet
- Zero email synchronization between your tablet and your computer
    - Having to delete the same email on all the devices you own
    - Can't save a message in a folder and have it show up elsewhere
- Having to periodically "unclog" your mailbox by logging in to webmail and deleting all the copies of everything you've already dealt with
- Can only see a few recent messages while on vacation checking webmail
- If you're using POP mail, and your computer's hard drive dies, guess what? Your messages were stored in your hard drive, so you've lost everything.

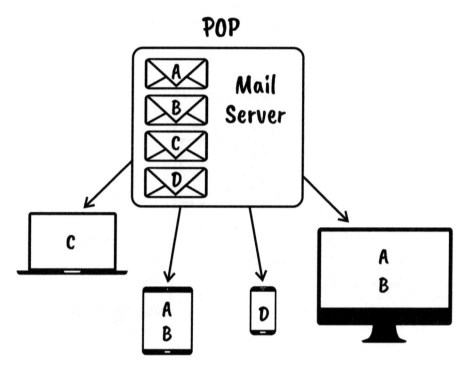

Additionally, you may experience:
- Zero spam protection
- If it's an email address your Internet Provider gave you, then you're dependent on that utility company for this email address, such as: JohnDoe@localcablecompany.com This causes a lot of people to remain with a lousy provider just to retain that address.

Back in 1988, people didn't have more than one computer. While you were "dialed in", the email server would throw messages at your computer like an angry paperboy, then you'd hang up. It's a one-way street. Fast forward to today, where one person owns multiple machines, and you'll have a discombobulated mess of summer messages. ("Summer here, and summer somewhere else!") Again, messages are then stored inside the individual devices, and in the event of a disaster, you've probably lost all of them.

What boils my blood is that people put up with all this, thinking *that's just the way it is*, and don't realize there's a better way.

IMAP

Slightly after 1988, a new form of email was invented that your computer guy probably hasn't heard of. It actually supports multiple devices! **IMAP** (Internet Message Access Protocol) implies a central email server that holds your mail for you. All of your devices (desktop, laptop, tablet, smartphone) simply VIEW the messages. So, if you delete a message, it's deleted centrally, so you don't have to delete it on each of your devices.

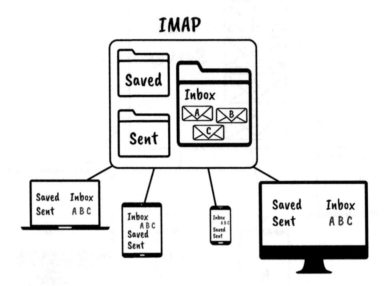

If your computer or tablet falls off a cliff, no big deal; your emails are still intact. If you buy a new PC, no problem; just sign in to your email account and *Bam!* you can see all of your emails. You have the ability to periodically archive your crucial messages into your local computer for safekeeping as well.

Spam

As far as Spam protection goes, ~~Hotmail~~, er, ~~MSN.com~~, er, ~~Live.com~~, er, Outlook.com, er, Whatever-Microsoft-renamed-it-to-this-week.com have "Mark Spam" buttons, but I think they send it to a tree-dwelling elf who just laughs and lets the spam keep flowing. Go ahead, check your grandma's AOL inbox too. It's overflowing with messages that are *obviously* spam, like misspelled Viagra, gift card, or diet pill offers. In contrast to this, I haven't seen a lick of Spam since I signed up for my Gmail account.

Mail Clients

There are two ways to read email on a computer: One way is to go to the provider's website, e.g. gmail.com or hotmail.com. The other way is to install a mail client in your computer.

Remember, a mail client is a program that allows you to read/write/organize emails. Mail clients can connect to both POP and IMAP email services. Examples of mail client software include Microsoft Outlook (disparaged earlier), Microsoft Windows Live Mail, the 1980s one-hit wonder Lotus Notes, Eudora, Apple Mac Mail, and the glorious Mozilla Thunderbird.

Mozilla Thunderbird is the open source alternative to those other products. Like many open source products, it strives to provide you a familiar experience, but works well. If you're familiar with Outlook, you'll pick it up in no time. Relative to the other elephants, it's insanely fast, isn't prone to self-corruption, and doesn't contain zillions of useless features. I've never seen a situation where it allowed a virus to gain access to your address book.

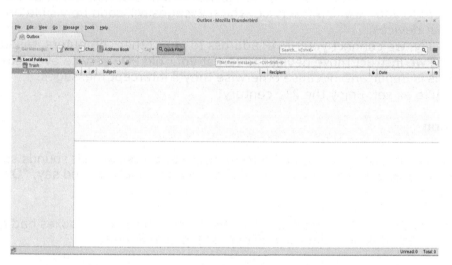

If you're using IMAP email already, it's very easy to switch to Thunderbird. Just install it, tell it you already have an email address, and give it your email address and password. You might need to consult your email provider for the IMAP server info. If you're rocking a POP address, keep reading.

The Exclusive Magical Transition Process

"Wait, but all my friends have my email address!"

My business offers a magical process that can rescue people away from POP seamlessly. So, let's say you're among the vast ocean of souls ~~suffering with~~ enjoying a Microsoft mail client and a free POP email address from your provider. Here's what we can do for you:

- Create a new email address, with a provider such as Gmail or Reagan.com. I recommend any IMAP provider that's independent from your Internet provider. **NO! You are NOT required to use the free email address your ISP gives you!**
    - If you're a small business owner, you'll want a web host like Starnova

that offers both a sitebuilder tool and IMAP email, so you can still be yourname@yourcompany.com!

- We then pipe any emails addressed to your old account into your new inbox, just like when you buy a new house and your postal service passes the mail on to your new address. Note that you do not have to tell your friends you have a new email address (although you should to be safe)! Once they send a message to your old address, it'll plop into your new inbox and you'll reply as your new name.
- Next, we connect your current mail client to your new provider. We can then *evacuate* your old emails that are locked inside that mail client and move them to your new IMAP service. The messages will soon be visible on all your devices.
- Finally, we connect your IMAP address to your other computers, tablets, etc. and we instruct those devices to forget your old POP service ever existed. This is important, because otherwise they'll intercept messages.
- You're all set. Enjoy the 21st century!

Encryption

Movies and journalists love using the term **encryption** because it sounds so mystical. After reading this section, you'll shrug your shoulders and say, "Oh, that's all that is?"

Remember eating *Cap'n Crunch* as a kid? Remember how cereal boxes had games on the back, like the word guessing ones? Let's play one now!

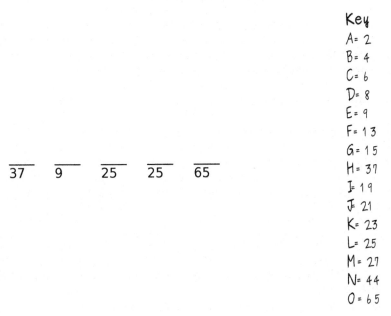

| 37 | 9 | 25 | 25 | 65 |

Key
A= 2
B= 4
C= 6
D= 8
E= 9
F= 13
G= 15
H= 37
I= 19
J= 21
K= 23
L= 25
M= 27
N= 44
O= 65

Got it? Good! That's encryption! That's all it is! If I want to send a message to me matey, and I don't want anybody else to understand what I'm saying, I can send that person an encrypted message, as long as I've shared that key with them beforehand. With encryption, I've swapped each letter in my message for another character. High-quality email providers use encryption to make sure nobody reads your messages as they're sent to your recipient.

Bonus concept: **Quantum computers** are on the horizon. They're made out of subatomic particles, and are so fast, they make today's best silicon CPU look like an abacus. With something so powerful, we'll soon be able to crack any encryption at all, very easily.[70]

Two styles

As you might imagine, if you send someone an encrypted message, the recipient has to know the key in order to make sense of the message you're trying to send. There are two ways to do this: In the first way, you share the key directly with them beforehand (that's how your home WiFi is kept secure).

In the second way, you both place your trust in a third party authority (which is how online banking is kept secure). Both your computer and the bank's computer "trust" each other thanks to an authority that provides the necessary keys. It's kind of like making friends at school: You don't know each other, but you can trust each other initially because you attend the same school.

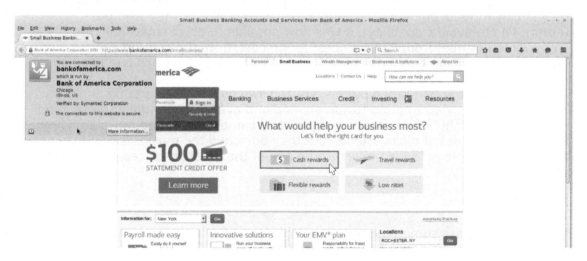

Click the green lock in your Web browser to make absolutely certain you're at the official website for your bank and that you're speaking securely through an intermediary authority.

Once you log in to your bank's website, nobody can see the information you exchange with your bank. So, the next time you hear a buzzword-laden radio ad trying to scare you into thinking that online banking over public WiFi is dangerous, you'll know better.

Most banks are insured to the gills, so I don't worry about banking online. Ironically, most of the cases I see are people who've been scammed *because* some Support Scammer called them and *scared them into thinking* their bank account was compromised!

DRM

When my nephew turned 1, his parents installed baby-proof locks on all the kitchen cupboards to keep him out. Ironically, he was the only one able to figure them out, and so the adults had to call him in to open up a door when it was time to make dinner! That's pretty much what happened in the story of **DRM**, which stands for Digital Rights Management or Digital Restrictions Management.

Around 1997, the public gained the ability to "rip" music from a Compact Disc onto a PC, and "burn" it back onto a blank CD. While boyfriends and girlfriends have made each other mixtapes for a generation, the digital nature of CDs meant that no matter how many times you made a copy, from CD to computer to CD, the quality was always identical.

These songs were now easily transferred from one device to another – I've coined the term **digitally liquid** to describe this. People started exchanging songs in a new way: Via **P2P networks** such as Napster. P2Ps didn't provide the music, but they simply introduced people to people who had the songs they wanted (attempting to avoid culpability). It was now possible to obtain material (copyrighted or free) from P2P services, for no cost, from the comfort of your own home. No more going out in the snow to pay $15 for a CD that has one good song!

The music industry, blindsided by this, started swinging its fists around aimlessly. They responded by attempting to sue anyone and everyone, including babies and dead people[17.] Eight trillion centuries later, they came up with another plan. They allowed online sales of digital media, but they poisoned the music with DRM, a copy protection technology that's proving to be one of the greatest pieces of ineptitude of the 21st century.

How DRM works

When you purchase something, it's yours forever, right? In the case of buying DRMed music/movies online, it's *encrypted*. Every time you press Play, your computer calls home to the retailer's website to ask if you have permission to listen to that song. If you have permission, and are using an authorized device to play it, it then unlocks the song with a hidden key. Most consumers aren't aware that this happens.

So what are we to do? On one hand, if we want to do the right thing, avoid being sued, and ensure the musicians receive compensation, we buy music online. We are then restricted as to where, when, and even how many devices we're allowed to use. Moreover, we can't loan music to family members anymore as we could with CDs & tapes, and on top of it all, we have to stay married to one retailer forever.

Encryption Schemes

Apple iTunes	Compatible only with iPods or computers running iTunes
Microsoft THREE music stores whose completely separate DRM schemes were *incompatible with each other.*[20]	<ul><li>MSN Music</li><li>Zune Music (required a Zune portable player)</li><li>Windows PlaysForSure (oh the irony)</li></ul>
Yahoo! Music	Who Knows
AOL Music	Who Cares

On the other hand, if we actually wanted to pirate something, we could go to a P2P service and get whatever we wanted. Whatever we download would already be stripped of its DRM: There would be no limit to how many copies, how many times we played the media, and absolutely no limit on what kinds of devices we could use to play it.

We all fall down

Remember, you're not renting the music; you're buying it. If you bought a car from a dealer that goes out of business, it's yours and you can still drive it. However, music/movies that are infected with DRM depend on the retailer to exist. *What could possibly go wrong!?*

Nothing at all, said the record execs.

Shortly after starting up, the AOL Music Store, the Yahoo! Music Store, The MSN Music Store, the Zune Music Store, and the Google Video store, all fell to pieces.[14] Remember, whenever you press play, your computer calls home to the retailer's website to beg for permission. Once those stores shut down, there was nobody answering on the other end. *All of the music that all of those customers purchased was rendered useless.*

The retailers actually *wanted* to grant the customers permanent access. However, a group of bumbling lawmakers created the DMCA, or Digital Millennium Copyright Act. That law makes it illegal to circumvent access control, regardless of the situational intent. According to that law, if the retailers had given their customers the encryption key to allow them to listen to their own music, they would've been found guilty of aiding and abetting piracy.

Let's say you purchased a car from the now-defunct Oldsmobile, Pontiac, Tucker, or Packard. On the day those factories stopped selling cars, did the car in your garage explode? Of course not; your car is yours. However, DRM has perverted our definition of ownership: Is what I just purchased really mine forever?

Same for eBooks

Remember Sony's eBook Reader? It was a beautifully crafted tablet for the purpose of reading electronic books. It debuted in the mid-2000s, one of the first of its kind. Upon its release, however, I predicted its failure: Books could only be purchased through Sony's online eBook store, which was encumbered with DRM. Guess what happened a few years later?

As announced by Sony, Reader Store in the U.S. and Canada closed on March 20, 2014, and customers were transferred to Toronto-based eReading company, Kobo. Accordingly, Reader Store accounts are now closed and access to purchased content is no longer available.[16]

I was able to snag a beautiful Sony Reader for $18 from someone whose collection was now defunct, and I populated it with DRM-free eBooks.

DVD Jon

VHS tapes play in any VCR that was certified for VHS. If you had the right set of magnetic parts, though, you could craft your own VCR and watch the tapes. Nowadays, when you play a DVD, you have to watch it on a player certified for DVDs. What's stopping you from playing it on an computer you built?

You guessed it: Commercial DVDs are encrypted, and can only be viewed by *authorized* players or software products (arbitrary region codes also dictate WHERE you can watch a DVD). A Norwegian teenager discovered this one day while trying to play a DVD in his computer, and he didn't like it. So he liberated *(decrpyted)* the content and copied it to his computer for his own personal enjoyment. He is now known the world over as DVD Jon.[21]

You can now purchase T-shirts with the DVD encryption key printed across the front (something like A=45 B=16 C=56) so you can help expose this illogical mess.

Note that DVDs are encrypted, but all DVDs are locked using the same key, and the player does *not* call home to Hollywood for permission before playing. Unfortunately its successor isn't so simple...

Dark side of the Blu

If you've watched a Blu-Ray movie, especially on a high-quality projector, you know how gorgeous the picture quality is. However, the movie industry didn't want to see another DVD Jon situation, so they cranked up the heat.

Blu-Ray Discs are encrypted with a key – but from time to time, the key is changed. So if and when the key is discovered, it'll only unlock movies released during the months that key was employed. Movies released before then will have a different key, and movies released after then will have yet another key.

What does this mean? Well, it means that pirates will be pirates, and they inevitably guess each key as it is released. More importantly, it means that each authorized Blu-Ray player must *call home* to get the new key whenever a new one is employed. This puts the burden of updating onto you the user, and you're paying for it: A portion of your purchase price funds the DRM. Plus, Lord knows what statistics Hollywood is reaping from your Blu-Ray player throughout the day.

We can now download HD movies from online retailers, so discs aren't really necessary anymore. However, both the Blu-Ray and the downloaded movie are going to be locked with DRM, so why bother buying an ungainly Blu-Ray player? I'll stick with DVDs, thanks.

Et tu, HDMI?

As you know, HDMI cables are the newest style of wire that connects Blu-Ray players, cable boxes, computers, and televisions. Since it's an all-digital method of transport, it delivers crystal-clear high definition picture and sound.

So why exactly is HDMI worse than its predecessors? The answer is **HDCP**. This industry guards its content so jealously, that these new cables now include anti-piracy technology called HDCP, (High-Bandwidth Digital Content Protection). The idea is that only authorized devices and accessories can transport the content. When you plug in an HDMI cable, it initiates a **handshake** that asks if the device is authorized to play that particular content. It's incredibly common for the handshake to malfunction (e.g. if the HDMI version is different, or the manufacturer didn't implement it quite right) and blow a false accusation of piracy. This is why we've all experienced an outage of picture or sound during an HD movie.

Here's the kicker: It's actually extremely easy for someone to pirate a movie, one way being to extract it out of an HDMI cable using $60 worth of adapters. Therefore, the ONLY way HDCP can activate is when it's a false alarm - when you are an innocent consumer who paid for your movie. HDCP is therefore completely incapable of preventing piracy, and proving to be an excellent method to penalize those who try to do the right thing.

Downloading vs. Streaming

Today, plenty of "all you can eat" services allow you to watch music and movies all day long for one very low monthly fee. Netflix and Pandora are two such pioneers from the mid-2000s. I'm a huge proponent of such services. In those cases, DRM is completely understandable. **However, if I stumble upon a show or a song I'd like to own forever, my hope is that I'll always be able to buy this media with no restrictions.** Not only would it ensure that we could enjoy those favorites well after everyone goes out of business, but it's also another revenue stream for them.

Hope

Steve Jobs' 2007 open letter to the music industry "Thoughts on Music"[18] destroys the argument for DRM. He notes that if there's anyone who would benefit financially from DRM and from forcing people to buy authorized music players, it's him! However, he was a genius and saw the big picture. (Remember our diagram earlier of the large grandiose wall with an unlocked back door!)

This issue could've easily devolved into a political gridlock (with people claiming that those of us against DRM were pro-piracy) had he not gone on to explain why DRM was simply unjust and ineffective against piracy.

Eventually, his Apple iTunes Music Store was able to strong-arm the music industry and offer most songs free from DRM, in the form of iTunes Plus. Walmart.com and Amazon.com also offer MP3s files completely free of DRM.

The compromise they came to is a very fair one in my opinion: No DRM, dependency, or restrictions are placed on your music. In order to discourage you from pirating, your email address is simply watermarked into the song. So if you do share it on a P2P network, they'll know it was you. It is my hope that video purchases will soon follow suit.

In conclusion, try to purchase non-DRM media, unless you're looking forward to a time when your entire investment is rendered unreadable. The same goes for software programs: Any program that phones home for "activation" means you can only install it while the company is in business. Oops.

Routers & Modems

A typical cable modem

And now for some fun stuff. A **modem** (short for modulator-demodulator) converts information for transmittal along a wire, such as a telephone or cable wire. It communicates with the modems located somewhere at your local Internet provider's office. Think of modems as the soup-can telephones we made as kids!

In the 90s, your dial-up modem connected your individual computer to your Internet provider via your Plain Old Telephone Service. Nowadays, a modern cable/DSL/fiber modem can connect you to the Internet at great speeds.

A typical wireless router

You can use a whole house full of computers and devices thanks to **routers**. Routers are responsible for doling out your Internet connection to all of them. They also bring your devices together so they can share information such as wireless printing. We'll discuss how they work in a bit.

Combo Boxes

Many ISPs will try and rent you a single wireless combo box, thus saving you the hassle of setting something up. Combo modem-router devices are inherently inferior, performing both functions poorly. If you're duped into renting a combo modem-router device from your cable company, here's what you're up against:

- You'll pay a monthly modem rental fee, and sometimes another wireless fee.
- Since they're jacks of all trades, most have far fewer features than a standard router. Many won't allow you to print wirelessly in your home.
- The wireless range on rental combo boxes is pathetic, usually not reaching farther than 20 feet. If you have a big house, you're screwed. (Some technicians don't know this, so rather than replace the combo box, they implement a complex grid of repeaters.)

A typical combo box

- They oftentimes use 1990s wireless encryption methods, meaning you're less than safe, and you have to memorize a hideously long password, like 45AASDASASF043950943594509ADASD903594390ABCDDF4395000000000 000000.
- Some installers don't even bother telling you your combo box has wireless functionality, or they mention it but fail to provide you the password for it! This happens more often than you'd think.
- Every router on the planet can handle at least 100 devices at a time, but I've seen combo boxes from many cable companies that limit you to 8!
- If you change Internet providers, you'll have to get a new combo box, set up a new password, and reconnect all your devices/printers/phones/etc.
- You may notice a second or even third wireless name broadcasting from within your house. Those are advertisement beacons your Internet provider injected into your combo box. This allows their other customers to utilize *your house* as a WiFi access point. They usually isolate that traffic from yours, but allowing people to sit in your driveway and use your Internet connection is not cool.
- All in all, the wireless combo box is rented out by companies that hope you don't know any better.

You should always *buy* a separate modem and separate router so you can avoid all of these hassles! (I avoid Linksys, as my recycle pile is populated with 1 and 2 year old units that overheated and cooked themselves. Their customers are also led to believe they need to install a "Setup CD" that wreaks havoc on PCs.)

And now you know how to protect yourself from your ISP.

How The Internet Works

What's an IP Address?

TV script writers and Support Scammers alike have used the term **IP address** to give us thrills and chills. Let's learn what this concept actually means. An IP address is simply a "phone number" or numerical name for any device connected to the Internet. Every home, office, website, device, etc. has one. An IP address is simply four groups of numbers, separated by dots, like this:

1.2.3.4

It follows one simple rule: Each of the four numbers must be between 0 and 255. So, the lowest IP address is 0.0.0.0, and the highest is 255.255.255.255. If you see some "hacker" on a crime show type in something like 256.360.560.400, that's not a valid IP address, is it?

Public vs. Private

There are two types of IP addresses - **Public** and **Private**. A public IP address is the number your building (household, office, hospital, etc.) shows to the outside world. A private IP is the number your devices go by while underneath that roof. Think of it this way – The Smith family lives in a house; they all share the last name of Smith; to the outside world they're known as the Smiths; however, each of them also has a first name that's used when talking amongst themselves inside the house.

Public vs. Private IP Addresses

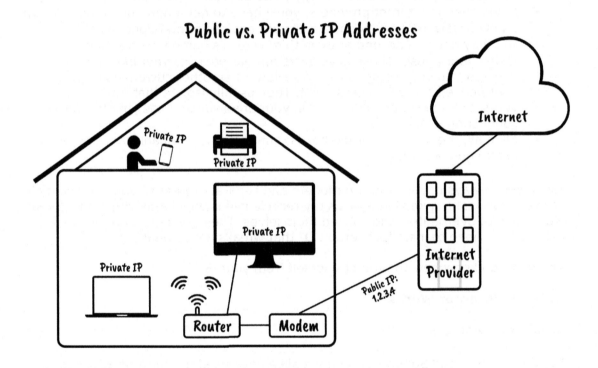

Public

Note that household public IP addresses change every time you reboot your modem (such IP addresses are known as **dynamic**). So, if a scammer says they can "see your IP address" - they're just telling you the number your modem shows the outside world on that given day – In essence, they're using a buzzword to try and scare you. Your router has a firewall built in, so as long as you *do not download the remote-control tool that they'll urge you to download,* they can't touch you.

For larger businesses, they reserve a public IP address that never changes (these are called **static**). This way employees can "dial in".

Running Out?

Recall what you learned about the limits of IP addresses. Each group has 256 different possibilities, and there are four groups. The number of possible combinations is therefore 256 times 256 times 256 times 256. That's around 4.2 billion addresses. Is that going to be enough for all the homes, offices, and websites in the world? You guessed it... we've run out. What do we do now?! The answer is IP version 6. IP version 6 has room for 340 undecillion addresses. Yes, that's a real number, and it's huge.[27]

Private

Each PC, mobile device, and Internet-connected gizmo inside your house is given a private IP by your router every time it's turned on. Residential device IP addresses are usually dynamic (changing with every reboot).

Rather than you having to worry about what devices have what IPs, there's now an easy way to get all your stuff talking to each other. The technology is called **UPnP** (called Bonjour in the Apple world). Instead of having to know the IP addresses of your wireless printers, your computer can now search for and summon them by a code that's basically a serial number. Think of it this way – if you lose touch with a friend and they change their phone number, you can still search for them on Facebook by their given name!

Computers and printers within offices are given static private IP addresses, to ensure the IT staff can send commands to all of them.

What is DNS?

When you're hungry, but you can't remember the phone number for The Pizza Chef, what do you do? You open a phonebook or call Directory Assistance, of course. They'll tell you what number to dial. That's basically how **DNS** works! It tells your computer what IP address a website resides at.

Let's say you want to visit ebay.com, subaru.com, teknosophy.com, or some other wildly popular website. Remember, every computer & website on Earth has a numeric IP address. So, how do we know what number to dial when we're hungry for some information? We type in the web address and our computer asks a DNS server for us! You type in ebay.com and your computer asks a DNS server "Hey, what's the number for this?" and a split-second later, it tells your computer to dial something like 12.34.56.78. That's it!

This way, eBay or Amazon or Subaru can change servers, change Internet providers, etc., and all they have to do is notify a DNS server that they're located at a new IP address.

Here's the beautiful thing about DNS: It's decentralized and redundant. If you tell one DNS server that your website is moving to a new IP address, they all start informing each other. It's sort of like they're gossiping!

If Heaven forbid half the world blows up tomorrow, the Internet will still work for those of us who remain. (Power grids work this way. So do earthworms, for that matter.) Nobody owns the Internet, nobody controls it centrally. That's why it works so well.

The Underbelly of Online Video

Net Neutrality

Anyone with a good Internet connection has little need for cable/satellite subscriptions anymore. Since video can now travel over the Internet, a distribution middleman is no longer necessary or relevant. Networks like HBO and ESPN, as well as niche Internet channels, are now offering customers direct Internet subscriptions with no cable company required! Imagine being able to receive water, milk, beer, soda, and fruit juice out of your kitchen faucet. You'd fire the milkman, wouldn't you?

Cable companies such as Verizon, Spectrum, and Comcast will continue offer both TV and Internet services. Soon, though, we'll just get Internet from them, and watch whatever we want over the Internet instead of only the channels they offer. In May of 2015, Comcast's Internet subscriptions surpassed their cable subscriptions for the first time.[28]

How are these failing giants reacting to this?

First, they started forging deals with traditional TV providers in order to keep their grip on those channels. Before you're allowed to watch Internet content from traditional providers such as CNN or FOX, you have to sign in with a username/password to prove that you're a customer of your local cable company! That middleman password ensures you can't watch those sites unless your local cable provider gets a cut, even if you're connecting directly to the content source far away from your hometown. That's like buying some aspirin while on vacation, and being approached by your home pharmacist, asking for his cut.

Second, they decided to peer into the pipeline going to your house and determine what you're doing with your Internet connection, then charge you based on that! So, if you're watching a video rather than reading a news page, the charge would be different. Imagine airport security asking you for money whenever you bring home an expensive gift.

Third, they strong-armed the new Internet video providers like Netflix and Hulu into paying arbitrary tolls, even though those video sites already pay their own Internet providers![86] That's like buggy-whip makers asking car companies for money.

The fight for **Net Neutrality** aims to stop the last two activities. The argument is this: The Internet should be a neutral pipeline. Internet providers, no matter how greedy they may be, have no right to peer into what you're doing and charge you or your content providers based on that. Fortunately, many brand new companies are delivering high-end fiber optic Internet connections to homes, and those companies usually aren't as invasive. To learn more about Net Neutrality, check out the Electronic Frontier Foundation.

Not Very Smart

Let's focus on Smart TVs now. They allow you to enjoy a handful of Internet video sites on your large living room television. Sound great, don't they? Those who buy them are unaware of what the term means. Smart TVs are televisions with itty bitty computers embedded inside them, which deliver those familiar computer traits you've come to love:

- Crashing
- Nagging
- Lagging
- Attacking for Updates
- Spying on what you watch[85]
- and adding a new dimension:
- Limiting you to certain Internet channels.

Each manufacturer's Smart TV interface is unique: Totally inconsistent and completely ultra-proprietary. Even I am dumbfounded by most Smart TV interfaces. The original goal behind a Smart TV was to help you enjoy Internet content on your large television, but rather than abide by some sort of universal standard, each manufacturer includes only a handful of its preferred apps. So, your Smart TV may offer the ability to watch Netflix, Hulu, and MLB, but fifteen minutes from now, when a new Internet channel out, you're unable to watch it.

Samsung Smart TVs actually have microphones in them that hear what you say in your house throughout the day and pass it on to one of their vendors. (Go ahead, research it. I'll wait here.) Technically it's legal, because they'll admit it in the fine print. How many of you would have purchased that TV if you had known? How many of you expect eavesdropping to be a function of a television?

Just like the car industry, the manufacturers really should stick to making the hardware and resist getting involved in the infotainment part. Apple, Google, and Amazon started feuding with each other recently, and as a result, are forbidding their customers from accessing each other's products. They'll only get away with this if we let them.

The computer industry has made this mistake before:

Peace, My Brother

When I was in high school, I wanted my own PC badly. I couldn't yet afford one, so my impatience led me to the 1996 Brother Super Power Note "laptop".[29] This unit was not at all a standard PC – it was a proprietary device, running its own proprietary Operating System with a tiny monochrome screen, and could only perform a dozen functions forever. (Basic word processor, calculator, Tetris, etc.) I quickly realized this and returned it, eventually buying myself a customizable, more all-purpose desktop PC.

Consider again the 1990s dialup online service. Their goal was to keep all their customers under their ultra-proprietary "walled garden" umbrella. They wanted everyone in the world to subscribe to this service, and visit the in-house "AOL keyword" services. As an added bonus, you could also go out into the "wilderness" of the Internet, which of course won out in the end due to its universal nature.

Such is the way with Smart TVs. EACH MANUFACTURER of Smart TVs wants you to be beholden to its own little world, and kept unaware of the entire world's worth of online content. (It also doesn't help that many content providers only work with a few specific brands of TV or mobile device rather than offering universally-accessible channels.) The moral of the story is: **Why buy something that limits you?**

If you are against people spying on you and dictating what TV apps you can watch, then avoid purchasing a walled-garden one-trick pony Smart TV. (If you have one, ignore its smart features and leave it disconnected from the Internet.) Then, buy yourself a more all-purpose Internet video appliance, such as Roku, Amazon Fire TV, AppleTV, or Streamplicity.

Unfortunately, silliness like this happens in the early adoption stage of a new industry. You may recall the TRS-80, Commodore, Apple][, Adam, and Atari platforms all vying for attention. Things eventually settle down into a more standard situation. The freedom to choose your own all-purpose devices and subscribe to any networks you like is ideally the future. We'll discuss more in the next chapter!

Zeroing

Let's say you'd like to re-sell your computer or mobile device. Not so fast! In the case of smartphones/tablets, you can perform a Factory Reset before selling your device. In theory that should destroy your personal information to a reasonable degree, but check with the manufacturer to be sure. (I've heard tons of stories where people who've purchased used cell phones and laptops can see all the personal info of the previous owner!)

In the case of a computer or laptop, you can usually remove the hard drive and physically destroy it. Many people find it fun to take it to the gun range!

However, there are instances where you wish to wipe a computer's hard drive without destroying it. Sometimes it's very difficult to remove a hard drive, such as in the all-glued-together iMac. In other cases, you'd like to destroy the information but keep the hard drive in a usable state, such as when re-selling a machine.

In these cases, we use *zeroing*. Think of it like this:

The quick brown fox ~~jumps over the lazy dog.~~

Imagine writing your name in pencil on a sheet of paper. If you erase what you wrote, you can pretty much make out what used to be written there. Such is the case with information on a hard drive/external drive. When you delete a file or even empty your Recycle Bin, your computer simply slaps a "condemned building" sticker on the file. For all intents and purposes, it's still there, and is visible by forensics experts with the right software tools. Most computer guys do a basic wipe like this and assume you're fine.

Zeroing means we write something else over the space we just marked for deletion. (There's no better way to get rid of a condemned building than by knocking it down and putting another up in its place!) It's now much harder to read what used to be there. When we command a computer to zero-out a hard drive, it writes the number zero over the entire hard drive completely, writing over any information that was there.

Zeroing once provides reasonable coverage, but the more you do it the better. According to Apple's Disk Utility, the US Department of Defense recommends performing this zero process *seven times in a row*, to shield your data from even the greatest forensics experts.

The History of Firefox

Most of us remember the battle between the early web browsers: Internet Explorer vs. Netscape Navigator. Microsoft started including IE free with every computer, and subsequently won out. Antitrust courts were not pleased.

Just before AOL gobbled them, Netscape released its its web browser as Open Source![19] Yes, it released the blueprints to the public. This allowed for unlimited modification and redistribution, as long as credit was given. It also ensured that the product will live forever! It's as if your favorite restaurant gave out its recipes the day they closed their doors.

This event spawned the Mozilla Foundation, which later created the Mozilla Firefox we know and love. This came back to bite Microsoft really hard, as the Firefox browser continues to take market share away from the near-defunct Internet

Explorer and its offspring Edge.

Targeted Advertising & Facebook

Email Ads

Targeted advertising is a two-sided coin. By tailoring advertising to specific audiences, consumers receive advertisements that are relevant to them, and the advertiser receives a better value for their advertising dollar, knowing the ads will be sent to those who are more likely to care. Why peddle computer parts to grandmothers, or crochet supplies to teenagers?

The issue is *how* we find out your statistics. How do we know you're X years old, of Y gender, enjoy reading A, B, and C, and even vote for Z party consistently? The websites you frequent can either ask you to volunteer your information on day one, or they can look through your browsing history as you go about your day.

Primitive email providers spew giant ad banners and videos all over your screen while you're trying to read email, and allow almost anyone to bombard you with spam throughout the day. Many are also hacked constantly. *Five hundred million* Yahoo accounts were breached in 2014[75] and another billion were discovered shortly after. (That is not an exaggeration.) The most helpless among us use such email services and have to deal with this.

Gmail, on the other hand, has computers (not humans) who scan your messages for keywords, and then display them in very small, one-line ads on the top of your screen while you're reading your mail. I remember writing an email to someone containing the word "invention" and a while later the ad on top announced a local patent attorney. Intrusive? Maybe, but in my opinion, a quiet line of text is a small price to pay for the best major email service around that has a near perfect spam filter.

Facebook

Facebook is a very interesting case. They ask you things on day one, such as your age, gender, and relationship status. They'll also look through the content you post on the site, and the communication between you and other members within the site. This enables them to display relevant ads on the side and in your News Feed. They can also *infer* your interests just by learning a few facts about you. Someone who clicks Like on a firearms page may receive ads from conservative groups, whereas someone who clicks Like on an environmentalist page will be presented with liberal ads. One day, after setting my own relationship status from dating to single, various dating services popped up immediately.

My opinion: Facebook is a great way to reconnect with people from long ago and far away. That being said, I try and limit my time on Facebook, since it's devolved into political browbeating[64], information harvesting, notifications galore, and those **clickbait** sites ("You won't believe what weird trick this single mother did to whiten her teeth car insurance belly fat Obama mortgage!").

Direct access to your brain

As the book *Dune Messiah* reminds us, an oppressed people welcome a new ruler, but discover that the new ruler can get out of hand, too. We're just getting over crashes and now we have to deal with notifications.

Lately you may have noticed everyone and his brother is making a smartphone App. This is because Apps have direct access to your phone's notification system... and consequently, access to you. Smartphones now dragoon us with dings, bings, and rings 24 hours a day, begging for our attention so we never get any work done.

If you're sick of this, you can go into your smartphone's settings and tell each App not to nag you anymore. I wouldn't have it any other way!

Digital Cleansing

People have begun to realize that companies are harvesting details about consumers[85] (location, habits, etc.) either for marketing or surveillance purposes, and storing it in a form known as **metadata**. Hence the rise of **digital cleansing**, where people flush records of their online activity.

Bet you didn't know this: Google records everything their customers search for, every site they go to, and every YouTube video they watch. People made aware of this have begun "flushing" their metadata from from Google (google.com/history) and turning off future monitoring. Similar processes are possible in the Windows 10 Privacy menu, and in Facebook, and so on. Whenever the news reports a tech company doing something unsavory, business surges over at the offices of DuckDuckGo, a search engine that pledges privacy to its users.[71]

Ideally, we'll have a choice between free services with targeted ads, and paid services that leave us completely private.

The Evolution of the Web

In the late 20th century, university, military, and eventually consumer computers came together to form the Internet. The World Wide Web (invented by Sir Tim Berners-Lee) became the great standard platform on which to display information to users around the world. A website can contain as many web pages as the owner wishes.

A web page can cross-reference any other web page in the world – just click on the reference (known as clickable links or hyperlinks) and your web browser takes you there! Think of your first paper encyclopedia: The article on F.D. Roosevelt might say "See World War II, Page 540". In this way, pages are linked to each other every which way and form a web of connections.

The earliest websites in the 1990s contained static (unchanging) pages where you could read articles or marketing information. In contrast to that, **Web 2.0** sites allow reader participation. The first example came as forums where you could have discussions on anything from car repair to movies. Next came social media, where you could reconnect with old friends and have endless political debates with them until you stopped talking to each other all over again. Stay tuned to our Future section to hear about the next step - crowdsourcing and user-generated content!

Memes

Oh, and let's not forget **memes** – "inside jokes" shared among Internet dwellers that parody a pop culture character. Memes are funny pictures that circulate around the Internet, where any individual can add his or her own caption! They can emerge from a popular cultural faux pas, a Web forum discussion gone awry, or any number of things.

For example, in 2009, Kanye West interrupted Taylor Swift during an award acceptance speech. Today, all across the Internet, you can find pictures of him taking her microphone, with a caption of "I'mma let you finish, but..." and whatever joke the Internet user wants to add to that.

One of my personal favorites is American Flag Shotgun Guy. It's a candid photo of some American expressing his patriotism. So now, all across the Internet, this photo exists with many different captions.

Here are a few classic memes[30], with some of their better captions.

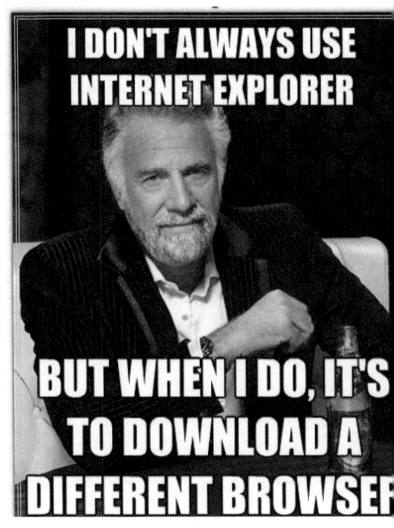

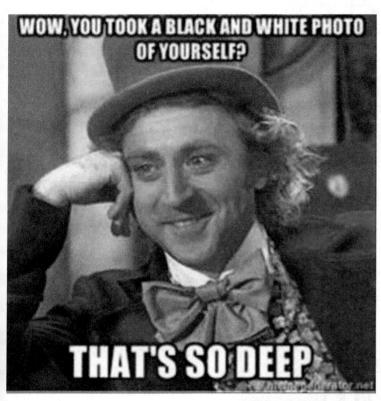

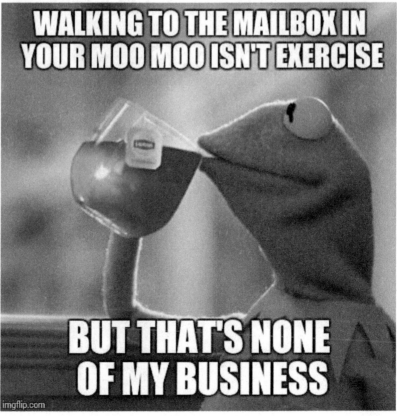

131

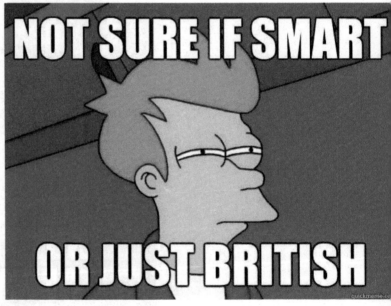

Clickbait articles

Anyone who's used the Internet has seen one: "TOP 10 CAST MEMBERS FROM THAT 80s SHOW TALKING TO AN 8 YEAR OLD DID FOR THIS SOLDIER AND HIS STUNNING SINGLE MOTHER WHILE OBAMA CALLED FOR SAVING MONEY ON THEIR HOME LOAN'S BELLY FAT!"

If you click on one, here's how the next 20 minutes of your life goes:
- You click on the link.
- 10 minutes later, the website loads, with some tantalizing intro.
- As you start reading, 400 trillion pop-ins get in your way, asking you to SIGN UP NOW FOR INFINITE SPAM UPDATES FOREVER FROM OUR UNKNOWN DESPERATE WEBSITE! Meanwhile, 90 ad videos start playing in the background.
- Once you swat those away, you read the intro, and realize you have to click Next Page to read each paragraph. Why? So each page can load more advertisements, videos, and pop-ins, of course!
- You'll realize you learned nothing meaningful.
- Someone made a few cents off of the whole deal.

More Cool Tips

Reboot Weekly

You must reboot everything you own once a week, and whenever you have an issue. This includes computers, laptops, smartphones, tablets, and the like. Routers and modems you can reboot monthly or when you have an issue. This prevents lots of problems, and usually saves you from having to call tech support!

In newer Windows machines, it is important to know that "shut down" no longer flushes the RAM, but rather hibernates the machine (perhaps in an attempt to impress you with how fast it performs its fake shut down). Therefore you must click "Restart" weekly otherwise your RAM isn't flushed.

Three Blind Laptops

Most new laptops come with bright LED screens... but why does your new laptop look so *dim?* The answer is, most laptop manufacturers crank down the brightness in a feeble attempt to "save the environment". LED screens are so efficient, that the savings are negligible, so the end result is people are going blind for no reason. Go into your laptop's control panel and crank up that brightness. You'll be amazed at its potential.

Surge Protection

Check under your desk. Chances are you have a plug strip for all of your equipment. You think it's going to protect you from power surges caused by lightning, right? Isn't that what those things do? Not so fast, Buckeroo. Grab a flashlight, and look all around it very carefully. If you don't see the word SURGE on it anywhere, then it's a fake! Fake ones usually call themselves Relocatable or Temporary Power Taps. Make sure you've purchased a real surge protector, and if you're extra cool, you'll buy a metal one, which of course won't burn as easily as a plastic one in the event of a lightning strike.

Darn you, Autocorrect!

Rather than improve those maddening little touchscreen keyboards, smartphone makers employ **autocorrect** helpers. Autocorrect can put words in our mouths that we never wanted, oftentimes sending people sentences that are nonsensical. (There are websites that chronicle the most embarrassing ones.) No need to worry! It's possible to go into your smartphone's settings, then go to keyboard or input settings, and turn it off!

Laptop Batteries

Laptop battery not as good as it used to be? You can call up the manufacturer and get a new one for $100, or you can grab one on Amazon or eBay for around $12. This book just paid for itself, eh?

Bluetooth

Bluetooth is a wireless technology that allows laptops, desktops, earpieces, headphones, cell phones, car stereos, home stereos, smartphones, tablets, video game controllers, keyboards, and mice to talk to each other. You can use Bluetooth to share files, play music on living room speakers, hold phone conversations using your car stereo, or even flirt with people inconspicuously in the Middle East!

It is thankfully an industrial standard, so Bluetooth-enabled devices of *any* brand can communicate. Imagine that! Its non-proprietary nature means adoption is easy and free of uncertainty, and we are constantly devising new uses for it. (Secret bonus tip: All it takes is a $20 adapter to turn your expensive home stereo into one capable of receiving music from your devices via Bluetooth!)

The various companies involved were initially unable to come up with a unique name. After a conversation and a beer, two engineers provisionally named the project after the Danish king Blåtand. (Pronounced "Blootand", anglicized as Bluetooth.[31]) Blåtand, whose name suggests he suffered from a dead blue tooth in his mouth, Christianized and united Scandinavia in the Middle Ages. Interesting, huh?

Reader Mode

Are you sick of massive video ads bogging down your machine when all you want to do is read a news article? Firefox offers a secret: Reader Mode. When reading an article in Firefox, a tiny book icon will appear in the address bar. Click it, and it strips the news article of everything and drops just the text on your screen. Brilliant.

Can of Air

Yes, they sell cans of air at most grocery stores. You should buy one, in fact. Every six months, squirt the pressurized air into all the fans on your desktop or laptop to get rid of all the dust. If a machine gets too dusty, it overheats and cooks itself!

Raspberry Pi

Buy your kids a Raspberry Pi. It's a FOSS-oriented, all-purpose, pocket-sized computer. They're great for learning computer engineering, great for creating projects, and they're not centrally controlled by anyone!

Recycling

Electronics usually contain lead, glass, precious metals, or toxic materials, so it's very important that we recycle them. With the dramatic increase of smartphones, throwaway printers, and factory-dependent cloud devices that die when the factory does, we've got to make sure to recycle our stuff.

Most towns offer some sort of pick-up program, and there are also many independent guys who will recycle your stuff for you. I love handing stacks of HP laptops to my recycling guy so he can melt them down.

Chapter 7: The Future

"The development of full artificial intelligence could spell the end of the human race." - Stephen Hawking[66]

In the 80s and 90s, we were hopeful for the future. Technology was supposed to get better and easier. Now, with things like DRM movies and Microsoft's GWX Intimidators, the computer nerds control the things we depend on. Some products de-improve, and things are becoming more confusing and intrusive. Some things are starting to look like *Running Man* or *The Fifth Element*, aren't they?

Shooting Squirrels with Bazookas

I usually work with senior citizens who are just getting into computers. Any initial setup was done by their kids or the jokers at the cell phone store, so they have no record of any passwords. They're overwhelmed as it is, and tech companies are making it worse.

When users forget their iPad's numeric passcode, the powerful anti-theft features kick in, and it turns itself into a pumpkin, er, paperweight. The only way you can ever use it again is by entering the user's iCloud account and password... assuming you know it.

If you forget the password, you have to call Apple and only Apple. (Independent IT technicians and locksmiths are now obsolete: The lock is centrally controlled!) Much of the time, whoever set up the iCloud account didn't bother to provide Apple with enough identifying information, such as credit card or phone number. (Nobody in the history of the world has ever remembered creating a Security Question, but companies love asking them.)

In the best situations, you're locked out temporarily. In the worst ones, you're denied access to your device and/or photos forever. When I confronted a phone representative about it, he responded "Well, our accounts are more secure than others." By that logic, security can only be achieved by welding your front door shut!

(In contrast to this, smarter companies will be more flexible, logical, and accurate in verifying your identity. if you lose your Gmail password, they will sometimes ask you for some names of the people in your address book, or the names of people you've communicated with recently. Facebook will show pictures of your friends, then ask you what their names are.)

I predict (and fear) that the pushy computer companies will start encrypting people's computer hard drives. Sure, it means that the machine is unreadable in the rare event of a theft, but for the 105% of users who forget their passwords, their data will be lost forever.

This ultra-centralized and overkill implementation of anti-theft tech is more of a thorn in our side than anything else. However, these centralized cloud companies have to create the semblance of security, because they're now responsible for all of this data that they're holding! Nobody's carrying nuclear secrets on these things. The *real* problem is people forgetting their passwords.

Software as a Rental

The software industry is pioneering a rental model, for better or worse. Rather than pay, say, $1000 for a program one time, you might have to pay $75 per month. Thus it's more affordable and will bring more customers to the table. Looks good at first, but remember, you pay that monthly fee *forever*, or you lose access to the product. They justify this by force-feeding a constant influx of new features you didn't ask for.

They claim you'll save money versus purchasing a new version every year – but who said you wanted any new features anyway? How many update attacks are meant not for security, but for the *job security* of the designers or marketers? At its worst, software rental isn't planned obsolescence, it's forced obsolescence.

In Microsoft's case, they've spared us from the whole affordability bit. They're charging $99 per year forever, for the Microsoft Office product that's available for a one-time purchase of $149![82] (I think I might start a car dealer that rents people cars for $40k a year!)

In the prior model, a new product upgrade came out, and you decided whether or not that upgrade was desirable it to you. The perceived value of an upgrade was perhaps higher then, because it cost money and the decision was completely in the customer's hands. Back then, software companies made money the old fashioned way, rather than resorting to leasing or data-harvesting models.

I for one enjoy one-time purchases (like most folks, my needs don't change much).

App Stores

Originally, a user could procure software directly from its author. One to one. Just between the you and the author. You evaluated the product, read some reviews, and downloaded it. (Note that if it's infected with DRM, then the program would only work until the day the author goes out of business.)

Then, those evil legal fake cleaners came out: They weren't quite viruses, but they deceived users hoping to clean their machines, and spied on them instead. How do we protect the average Joe from this? The answer is an App store. Those of you who have downloaded Apps on mobile devices have already used one, and it's coming soon to a computer near you.

An **App store** is a centralized software retailer website that *reviews each product's integrity* to ensure your safety before making it available. If implemented properly, it prevents the mass deception and flight of cash that the world has experienced with fake cleaners.

History

The Linux community pioneered the App store: Its users have at their fingertips a repository of popular programs. These repositories could be accessed anonymously, but new commercial ones require identification.

Launched as a component of the first iPhone, Apple brought this concept into the mainstream. With its iPod and iPhone, Apple culture grew into something beyond the small-town community it had historically been. An App store would enable them to keep tabs on what programs were being written for the iPhone/iPad (and how well they were written), not to mention skim off a few pennies from each purchase. The Apple App Store requires login identification, and is the *exclusive* source of software on the Apple mobile devices. (Imagine if you were *only* allowed to buy groceries at one market! Luckily people are starting to sue for the right to use alternative App stores.[79])

Facepalm

Microsoft's so late to the party, all the Doritos are gone. An App store platform is a chicken and egg situation: Enough people need to buy the devices, which is encouraged by the number of Apps available for the platform, and vice versa. After only a handful of people purchased Surface tablets, and fewer still have signed in to the Windows 8 & 10 App stores, Microsoft decided to pull two punches to boost their numbers:

- They lowered their standards on what they consider a valid App. A recent article[1] reports that the Windows App Store is chock full of fake apps, such as apps that "teach you how to download" other apps. This negates the entire purpose of an App store!
- A Windows App Store account controls access to the entire machine. If a bad guy signs in to one of your Microsoft devices, he could conceivably control all of them in one fell swoop!

Do you think there's any place in the future for such silliness?

When firing up a new Windows machine, they may lead you to believe you must create a Windows App Store account before you're allowed to use it. If you don't want to sign up, you have to humor them first by clicking "Create Account". On the next page, look for the microscopic "Leave me alone and let me continue with a Local account." button. If you're already using one, you can always go to PC Settings, then look for the "Disconnect" or "Switch to a Local Account" button.

The Third Door

Tai Chi students know the world isn't a one-dimensional sliding scale. We seek a third, more creative option to solve a problem without tradeoffs.[32]

My suggestion is to simply allow multiple App stores, like you see on Android devices. Yes, there's an official App store for most users, but experts can also install Apps via alternative App stores or even via a USB cord. Beginners are kept safe, and experts are left unrestricted.

The Internet of Headaches

Smart thermostats, TVs, phones, and even smart buildings: All of these sounded wondrous in 80s movies, but now, knowing what you know about this industry, are you still excited? Cloud hype has just ushered in the Internet of Things, that next great exercise in alchemy where people start rubbing the "technology salve" all over our perfectly good appliances.

IoT devices are smart gizmos, such as a thermostat connected to your home WiFi that you can control while you're out on the town. That's a lovely idea if you're an expert, but a tiny hassle is traded for extreme complication, unreliability, helplessness, and the ability for companies and thieves to harvest our behavioral data and control our devices.

As long as proprietary design, ultraconfusing installation procedures, shoddy programming, and privacy violations are minimized, these gadgets would deliver convenience and peace of mind. It could be convenient to have one or two well-thought-out electronics around your house that save you time, but there's no reason they have to be centrally controlled! This opens the door to disaster: In late 2016, an "army" of IoT devices were hijacked and re-programmed to attack DNS servers, causing Internet outages around the globe![65]

Billions of these hyperactive gizmos are about to be foisted onto consumers in the near future, claiming they'll be able to help us in our daily lives. Some of us are old enough to remember the first Home Automation craze of the 1980s – Were those cameras and intercoms ever used beyond movie props and conversation pieces? Are any of us still able to find parts for those old proprietary systems? Do any of them still work? (We're in for some deja vu: Cloud-controlled lights, doorbells, routers, etc. all rely on an App downloaded from an App store. Five seconds from now when the maker goes out of business, or tells you your device is "too old"? Landfill.)

The human compulsion to control each other is becoming easier to accomplish. This isn't a bubble waiting to burst, now is it? Raise your hand if you want the government to tell you how warm you can heat your home. How about WiFi-controlled front door locks? Anyone?

Baked-In Control

Since most IoT devices are closed-source, they're a "black box" - In other words, we have no idea what they're capable of, what they've been programmed to do, and who can get into their back doors to turn them against us. In "How Laws Restricting Tech Actually Expose Us to Greater Harm"[73], Cory Doctorow of WIRED magazine reminds us we're at risk of becoming beholden to black box devices. We'll be buckled into our seats whizzing around in cars with minds of their own, experiencing things far worse than the minor annoyances we've seen in the past 20 years. He illustrates a future bleaker than the one I have, where businesses and governments can bake in all sorts of regulations and back door **kill switches**. (Anyone who's raced at the local go-kart track knows the track owner can cut all engines off with one button.) His argument is this: If they penalize the disclosure of security flaws and back doors (like the recent one where a $40 computer part can be programmed to unlock over 100 million Volkswagens[74]), it doesn't stop malicious criminals from finding them, and ironically this ensures that only they will know about them.

Reminds you of our castle diagram, doesn't it?

The Workforce

Today, people drive us around in taxis, cash us out at the store, and help us bank. A buddy of mine claims he saw people in India cutting a lawn by hand, with scissors! From self-driving cars to self checkout aisles to ATMs (and even Pandora's music recommendations), the robots are coming. Automation sounds great at first, but it's not without fallout. First, it takes jobs away from nontechnical folks and assumes everyone in the world should become a programmer. Second, the high-tech workforce risks being too centralized (recall our one-way diagram). Third, the robotic world becomes too rigid and impersonal. Your experience with your banker, concierge, or music store hippy will always outshine tapping on a screen. Finally, once we've made self-enjoying walks on the beach and self-eating cheeseburgers, what's left? Virtual Reality games and cat videos? No thanks.

A few companies are even creating their own monolithic "deep mind" artificial intelligence computers. Not at all a disaster waiting to happen, is it?

Personal Cloud

Originally, computer storage and backup were linear. You had *one single computer* with some documents and photos, and if you were smart you backed up your data onto floppies or CDs periodically. Then came the cloud backup services (you know, Carbonite, iDrive, and Mozy), but they're still unidirectional. Standard online backup services are ONE-WAY backups (as opposed to synchronization services), meant for users of ONE single machine.

Synchronizing my current projects

That's all well and good, but what about those of us who own many computers and tablets and want to synchronize our work? I personally don't have use for a one-way one-machine online backup, since I have several computers. All these new machines, e.g. netbooks, ultrabooks, tablets, Chromebooks, and those other bizarre "cloudbooks" are geared toward synchronization services.

Being a member of a cloud **synchronization service** allows me to synchronize the contents of all my personal computers, whenever they're connected to the Internet. For example, if I edit a document on my laptop at a cafe, (I am now!), I can go to my home and office computers and see the same work reflected there.

Unfortunately newer tablets and cloudbooks are designed in the hopes that you keep your data in the manufacturer's own cloud service. When using a cloud synchronization service, I insist on using a *neutral/platform agnostic* one that isn't biased toward any one hardware manufacturer. Using a neutral one insures you are not locked in to any one manufacturer when it comes time to purchase another smartphone or computer! Examples include Box, iDriveSync, and my favorite Dropbox. (Careful, though, Dropbox pounces on any thumb drives and cameras you plug in. *HEY CAN I HAVE THESE PHOTOS?*)

Proprietary Sync Services vs. Platform Agnostic Ones

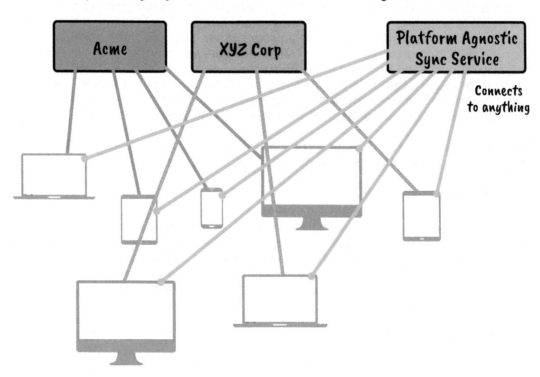

You can also use a synchronization service to keep all your small business machines up to date as well! This way your employees can be anywhere in the world, and still have the current company policy, documents, etc. If you do a cloud sync, you'll still want to back up this stuff to a local drive periodically. I never keep anything exclusively in the cloud!!!

My personal cloud server

I only store my current projects and photos on a cloud synchronization service. As for the rest of my user data, my archive of documents/photos/music/etc., I bought MY OWN PERSONAL SERVER (called a **NAS**) for my house. None of the individual machines hold my data. This way I can have 2 or 20 or 200 PCs in my house, and buy and sell them as I please.

NAS (I pronounce it as "Nazz") stands for Network Attached Storage. A NAS is simply a hard drive with an Ethernet jack on the back, accessible by any computer in my house, secured with an optional password. You can "map" them just like any other shared network drive, such as the Y: drive or the Z: drive. They're impervious to viruses in and of themselves (by virtue of being... oh, you know), and they're under $200!

This isn't your daddy's server, though. In the 1990s, small and medium sized businesses purchased Windows servers to act as their router, firewall, email server, domain controller, and network drive. You guessed it: When it went down, all of those functions were unavailable. Tragically, there are still jokers going around selling these Windows servers to tiny offices for $10,000 each because they are unaware of the existence of NAS devices (or ethics).

I *love love love* liberating small offices from those 1990s-style Windows domain servers and supplying them with real routers, NAS devices, and proper IMAP email. No more office-wide meltdowns, and no more massive IT expenses.

If a NAS is set up correctly, it will perform its own backups to its own internal "mirror", but I still do a proper USB backup to an external drive every few months to be extra safe.

NAS: Your Personal Cloud

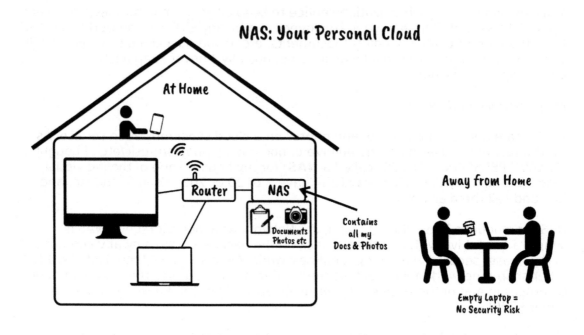

At Home

Router

NAS

Documents
Photos etc

Contains
all my
Docs & Photos

Away from Home

Empty Laptop =
No Security Risk

Some more good things: Disruptive Technology

e-Commerce

Remember those little hypothetical companies in your high school economics class? One town had a pizza factory and the other town had a robot factory, and they achieved efficiency by selling their goods to each other. Through **e-Commerce** websites, small businesses in any town on Earth can sell to individuals who need what they have! It ensures we can find the best service and the lowest price, no matter where it comes from.

You can create your own e-Commerce site, meaning one that is capable of inventorying, showcasing, and selling your wares to the world. Alternatively, you can sell alongside others on a connector site such as eBay, car-parts.com, or etsy.com. Hobbyists, collectors, repair people, you name it.

I can go online and buy parts to fix pretty much anything. Computer parts, car parts, TV parts, sewing machine parts, stereo parts, coffeemaker parts... saving them from the landfill.

3D Printing

If I can't find the car or gizmo part I need, I can now print it out. 3D printers spit out not sheets of paper, but real three dimensional objects, in either plastic or metal.

There are even companies offering to 3D print the custom car of your dreams! Beats all this proprietary factory-dependent malarkey. Talk about disrupting the gravy train.

VoIP

Remember, any form of information can travel over the Internet, including video or voice. **VoIP** stands for Voice over IP, in other words, carrying phonecalls over the Internet. You can use a VoIP line to call any normal phone number, at rates that are much cheaper than traditional phone lines.

VoIP companies, such as Vonage and MagicJack, provide you a real phone number thanks to a VoIP adapter that communicates with their website. The adapter goes between your router and the master phone wire in your basement, thus powering all the standard telephones in your house. I have one VoIP line that's only $40 *per year* for unlimited calls to the U.S. and Canada! (Some cable companies offer "digital phone" services to people who aren't aware VoIP exists.)

For some, traveling internationally *used to* mean significant cell phone bills. You (and unfortunately Support Scammers) can now take a VoIP adapter anywhere on Earth, because VoIP lines know no boundaries. While traveling abroad, T-Mobile and MagicJack customers can connect their smartphones to a hotel's/friend's/cafe's WiFi and call home all day long for free.

I still keep an old-fashioned real telephone line, because it's more reliable!

Online Maps

In 1998, Microsoft launched Terraserver. The idea was to "quilt" together satellite photos of the whole planet. Later, websites like MapQuest, Google Maps, and OpenStreetMap came about. (Google Maps has a cool feature where travelers can share their shots of the Eiffel Tower, sunsets, the Pyramids, and the like!) From these sites, you can now print out directions for your next road trip – no more requesting a custom map from your local auto club! Better yet, request directions on your GPS or smartphone, and stick it on your dashboard for real-time guidance! The debut version of the Apple Maps App helped people drive off of bridges, but now also features road directions.[57]

Streaming Music

Sure, I love to purchase CDs and restriction-free MP3s. But sometimes I want to know what's out there, what's new, or maybe just let someone else do the picking. In this case, there are a lot of options, such as:
- Pandora
- Spotify
- SomaFM
- SiriusXM online
- TONS of independent Internet radio stations

Each of these has a website and a mobile App. In the case of independent stations, you can either go to your favorite station's website, or browse a directory of them such as TuneIn or iHeartRadio. Do yourself a favor and connect your device to a decent stereo. I'm a huge fan of electronica and alternative music, but you can listen to any genre in the world online!

Crowdfunding

In the olden days, we asked our rich uncles to help us start businesses, and held pancake fundraisers for our sick friends. Nowadays, we have **crowdfunding**, where we can ask friends to pitch in a few bucks online. Startups promise their first line of prototypes to the first group of people who throw them money via Kickstarter, and people can help their friends with medical bills through sites like GoFundMe.

Education

Higher education's decline in value per dollar has collided with the Internet's ability to break down barriers. One can now easily achieve the equivalent of a college degree online for little to no money.
Check out:

- Ted.com – Actual geniuses from around the world delivering eye-opening lectures for free
- Khan Academy – Collaborative education, such as a detailed math course
- Gutenberg.org – Digitally preserving almost every public domain book in history, each one freely downloadable to your eBook reader
- Learner.org – Educational video series, such as Discovering Psychology
- EdX and Coursera – Major universities offering free online courses
- You can even take all the MBA classes from University of Illinois for free.

Tizen OS

Tizen is a new Linux-based Operating System, Samsung's declaration of independence from Google Android. I originally perceived Tizen as a fearsome update-mongering spy machine, but things took an interesting turn when I found out it was in the custody of a neutral consortium whose motto was: "An open-source, standards-based software platform for multiple device categories." Their design website teaches programmers how to avoid irritating and annoying users, and even details proper grammar usage! The OS has the capability of running Android apps, so there's no chicken and egg situation. It's even going to be used to power some automotive infotainment systems so we can have a little control over our dashboards again.[40] Sounds hopeful!

Ideally, we'll see mobile devices running Tizen, Firefox, and Ubuntu soon.

The Future of Television

Bill Gates wrote a book in 1994 called *The Road Ahead*. In it, he clairvoyantly predicted that we would someday have a single connection to our homes, that provided telephone, videophone, television, and other Internet services. He also predicted that we would eventually watch whatever we wanted, asynchronously (on-demand), from various servers located around the world. For the most part he was spot on, except for whatever reason, his company isn't really involved in much of it.

In 2008, I predicted the separation of content and delivery was at hand. From the 1970s until the 2000s, cable companies had been your exclusive link to specialized television programming. You know, Food TV, Comedy Central, the Oprah Winfrey Network, the Minnesota Fly-Fishing Network, the Chilean Underwater Basket-Weaving Channel, the Tibetan Mud-Wrestling Network...

Then along came the disruptive Internet. At first, capable of email, then news articles, followed by voice communications, and now video entertainment. Yes, Big Media's arbitrary national barriers are shattered. The Internet brings us television and radio stations from around the world.

It's fertile soil for **narrowcasting** and **crowdsourcing**. Narrowcasting means broadcasting over the Internet, reaching only those who are interested. Television shows like Firefly and Arrested Development had cult followings but failed on network television. Such shows do very very well on Netflix, which delivers *niche* television shows on demand to customers via the Internet. People don't write books to please everyone, and now they don't have to write TV and movies to please everyone either.

Furthermore, the low cost and ubiquity of the Internet means anyone with a video camera can now create a television show and place it on distribution platforms such as YouTube, Miro, or even Netflix. (There's Flickr for photographers and SoundCloud for musicians.) This is known as crowdsourcing or User-Generated Content: The creators of a UGC site simply lay the groundwork platform, and the users of the platform create and contribute the media for other users to consume. This means Hollywood and general interest TV shows no longer have a monopoly on our attention, and I predict most of the rising stars created in the future will come from UGC, which blissfully bypasses DRM and border restrictions.

So, if you connect your non-Smart TV to an external Internet video appliance, you'll be able to enjoy all the new niche content out there, from a huge variety of sources, regardless of the platform.

Streamplicity

We definitely need a method to enjoy all this Internet video on our huge televisions, as opposed to squinting at our tiny phones and laptop screens. There are many great devices you can connect to your television to achieve this. The problem is, what device do we use? There are a lot of good ones out there, and my company is diving into the fray with the Streamplicity set-top box. It connects to any television and allows you to watch just about any Internet content.
- We don't spy on you or dictate what you can watch.
- It allows for tons of accessories, such as gyroscopic remote control, wireless keyboard, home theater speakers, and almost anything else that obeys the Bluetooth, USB, or headphone jack standards.
- It comes with the Streamplicity App, which holds a sampling of different streaming television channels from around the world, free of charge. If you're an immigrant looking for news from back home, or would like to learn another language, you're going to love it.
- It's Android based, so you can watch any of the networks that already offer Android apps, such as ESPN, CBS, Hulu, YouTube, TED, Twitch, and a myriad of small/independent networks.

More information can be found at www.streamplicity.com .

Suggestions

Dear Automakers,

Many new cars these days come with unwieldy in-dash infotainment systems, as opposed to the old removable "double DIN" stereos. These systems offer pretty color screens, navigation, car telematics, and oftentimes additional services connected to the manufacturer. Almost all are unresponsive and confusing, and some are vulnerable[52]. That's all well and good, but apparently *nobody* in the car industry realizes that five seconds from now, new technologies will have made this week's in-dash navigation infotainment systems obsolete. At that point, those of us who purchased cars with these non-removable systems will be left holding the bag.

Let's talk about security for a minute. Bloomberg revealed a recent scandal where thieves could easily impersonate commands from a remote control keyfob to lock and unlock cars. But wait, there's more! For those of you who have Start/Stop buttons: "The implications of the attacks presented in this paper are especially serious for those vehicles with keyless ignition."[53] **Electronic wizardry means more exposure to theft.**

If autonomous cars become popular, I can completely understand the need for them to "talk" to each other ad-hoc. However, a car that obeys a central authority implies a single point of failure and exposure to bad guys intercepting control. Such a car is a dealbreaker for me. Centralized remote control is the goal of some engineers, who sometimes believe they can perfect society *if it weren't for those pesky individuals and their pesky free will!*

Surveys say most people are against automated cars. Why? The lack of trust.[58] I get that self-driving automobiles are the wave of the future, but don't try to eliminate the past with all the fervor of a Communist censor. Having a manual override will save lives and allow people to retain their trust. The automobile, after all, was meant to empower people, not to make them feel trapped and dependent. That's what buses are for!

If you want to earn people's trust, make products people actually want to buy: Upgradeable, repairable, and untethered.

Dear independent repair shops,

Even if you're a terrible technician, if you return phonecalls in a timely manner, you'll be successful. Most computer guys don't bother returning calls, for reasons no sociologist can surmise. Even if you hire someone just to return calls and tell people you're working on their case, it'll be well worth it.

Change your focus from constant viruses and patches to installation of solid products. I've discovered that customers are willing to pay for that privilege. The cat's out of the bag; it's only a matter of time before people move onto virus-free tablets, so why not be the one who liberates them? They won't need you as often, but boy will they tell their friends.

Dear mobile device manufacturers,

Eventually, enough people will lose enough money and enough photos on enough mobile phones, that they'll start to demand modular, repairable mobile devices. Environmentalists and cheapskates alike are sick of throwing our glued-together phones into landfills.

History books described how the miracle of interchangeable parts enabled us hunter-gatherers to live better lives. Beyond just parts within a product, imagine interchanging parts from any manufacturer! Google's Project Ara and Dave Hakkens' Phonebloks are refreshingly brilliant, because they propose precisely this. These projects propose an open architecture for mobile devices, similar to desktop PCs: A single standard platform of monopolistic competition where component manufacturers compete on equal footing. Just as computer gamers enjoy being able to upgrade and repair their rigs, the next generation of mobile device hardware and software should be more customizable.

Dear product designers,

When criticizing you I must keep in mind you don't realize what you're doing. I too have been guilty of scope creep (being too eager to increase the range of services I offer). New products are increasingly riddled with features, and less reliable and less intuitive. Such products perplex customers (even intelligent, successful people) and make them feel dependent on tech support, and we all know how much training those folks are given.

A lot of this headache is unnecessary. Rather than push unwanted products on people, find out what they actually need and study how they use your current products. Keep intuitive design and enjoyment of use in mind, rather than constant tidal waves of uncalled-for features. Creating simple, reliable products with more logical operations will remove the intimidation, the dependence, and the disdain for technology. Eventually people will trust you and abandon terrible products for your simpler ones if you make them available. *Learn* from the boneyard of failed products (Windows 8)!

Technology is NOT a panacea, or salve. There *is* such thing as over-saturating something with technology. Smart Fridges aren't going to help anyone. As they say in the books "The Island of Dr. Moreau" and "Jurassic Park", just because you CAN do something, doesn't mean you should.

In the past, having a proprietary product was a business goal. However, when it's taken to such an extreme that the products you sell depend on your existence, proprietary is unacceptable. Imagine being unable to repair your house because the builder went out of business!

Try to use industrial standards, stop using short-sighted thinking, and respect your user more. There's nothing wrong with making a lot of money, but don't do it by forcing people onto your gravy train. Use a little less greed and a little more common sense, and in the end you'll make more money anyway. Create a coherent business model and open up the protocols so others can join in and grow your idea. Only then will you be more successful.

Dear Apple,

Design products that play well with others. You only succeed when you do so, such as when you made the iPod available to Windows users, or when you released the Mac mini that uses standard parts and connections. Consider opening up your AirPlay and AirDrop standards – you have nothing to lose and everything to gain. There's a difference between people admiring you for your superior product and people who are forced to buy your product to remain in your ecosystem. Don't forget to look at the big picture, as Steve Jobs did so masterfully.

Listen to Steve Wozniak when he says the cloud will cause horrible problems. Don't think for a second that people depending on someone to hold their private information is somehow a good thing.[44] Take pride in the fact that you're the only commercially available computer that's oriented toward simplicity, free of bloatware, and virtually virus-free. You've got a lot of growth potential on the desktop.

I always poke fun at the PC industry for taking sometimes 10 years to adopt technologies you pioneered. I get that you want to be a progressive company, but don't deprecate things for the sake of it. The whole world still needs DVD drives, USB ports, and headphone jacks.[45]

Dear Microsoft,

In no other industry would your products be remotely acceptable. Windows machines are absolutely embarrassing, crashing and nagging before they even leave the retail display! Internet forum discussions (and landfills) are littered with PCs that physically function but hold corrupt copies of Windows that inexplicably gave up the ghost.

Most Windows PCs are loaded with gobs of bloatware from the hardware manufacturers. If you want to survive, why don't you make your (anti-bloatware) Signature spec mandatory?

I've had the pleasure of meeting some of you, and you're good, capable people. Instead of claiming the regurgitated Windows 10 is the final remodel of your flagship product, how about replacing it with something totally new, like that beautiful Singularity project you talked about in 2008? Bite the bullet and release something actually new, instead of yet another piece of Swiss cheese. Don't worry about interruptions and incompatibilities; each new version of Windows brings mayhem *anyway*.

Dear software designers,

Don't add things just for the sake of adding them. Another great example of a useless feature is the "suggestion attack" – When a user tries to log in to some website, the browser interrupts and suggests either various misspellings of usernames, or search recommendations. This feature is one of many that should've never been implemented. Avoid building Jenga towers or Towers of Pisa – sure they're getting taller, but are they going in the right direction?

Try to avoid arbitrary "helper" overlays that seek to assist people with one certain task instead of simply encouraging basic computer literacy (such as file management, copy-paste, and folder heirarchy). That's how we got into the massive quagmire of photo management programs and "download managers". Oftentimes those arbitrary helpers require you to rely on them forever, such as a hard drive infected with automated backup software.

Stop purging all the **skeuomorphs** (icons based on real life, such as shopping carts, floppy disk save buttons, or telephone handset icons). Just because these familiar symbols are antiquated doesn't mean they aren't badly needed.

Avoid "guiding" people to the outcomes you desire. It makes users feel manipulated, deceived, or at the very least disrespected. How many people have been caught off guard by Amazon Prime buttons, only to resent the company later? Remember, people will love you if you're honest with them.

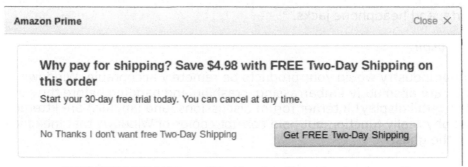

"YES SIGN ME UP" vs. "No thanks, I'm a bad person."

Windows 7 was well-liked because it undid most of the "new features" of its predecessor, and had a clean, familiar interface. I believe there are great rewards for those who make straightforward products – this is half of the reason for the success of tablets. It's a consideration you have to make every day, with every decision.

Remember, individuals and businesses actually depend on the stuff you make. If you focus on quality, people won't hate using computers.

Dear music and video industry,

Purchasing something implies the ability to use it forever. DRM violates that. Remember, it's like anti-theft retail packaging: It can only serve to penalize those doing the right thing. Find new ways to monetize things. Recall Disney's initial apprehension to the VCR, and the fortune that ensued after they opened their minds. People will always pick the easiest option, so if you make purchases easier than piracy, they'll do it.

Dear lawmakers,

Now you know what my industry's been up to. Nothing works as it should, companies are spying, and so on. Laws created for this industry can:
- become outdated too quickly
- be circumvented by the bad guys easily
- add barriers to entry
- end up hurting the small guy
- and subsequently encourage consolidation and monopolies.

Let's focus more on disclosure and letting the customer decide on the open market: Things like Net Neutrality prevent telecom monopolies from squeezing their customers based on what they're doing on the Internet. Things like the Fair Repair Bill actually protect us from companies that don't want consumers to repair the possessions we bought from them. Starting a discussion about the right to protect oneself from update attacks might be a good idea, too.

The purpose of a patent was to secure a company's right to make money off of an invention. I whole-heartedly support that. Recall that patents also ensured the public knew what was going on behind the scenes, how the product worked. Likewise, it might be a good idea for the public to be able to see software source code. Any malicious intent would be seen right away, and it ensures compatibility as well as repairability in the event that a software or car company ceases to operate.

We are at a crossroads. We must decide between a digital future that liberates us, or one that limits and harms us. Now is the time to lay the groundwork for the next generation of technology ethics: Software disclosure, Electronic Medical Records privacy, IoT security, neuroscience ethics, and genetic engineering ethics.

P.S. Why don't you go after the pornography industry with the same fervor you did the tobacco industry? You're welcome.

Dear Reader,

Hopefully you had a few laughs and now feel more confident with technology. As you know, there ARE some good things that come out of it, and hopefully the bad things will be short-lived.

You might even be brave enough to troubleshoot your issues by narrowing down the culprit: For example, if you can make photocopies on your printer but are unable to send a print request from your computer, there's nothing wrong with your printer; it's your computer or USB cord's fault.

Also, I appreciate customers who appreciate me. There are two types of customers – ones who whine when it comes to writing me a check, and ones who say, "Wow we're glad to pay you since you've saved us so much money and we have so few problems now!"

The examples used in this book will eventually become dated, but the concepts, principles, and advice are timeless. Human nature doesn't change. My hope is that you'll develop a good sense of smell when faced with desperate new products and scams. I don't expect you to agree with everything I say, but even if you use a pinch of this spice in your recipe, it'll be worth it.

If you don't enjoy paying for constantly-breaking technology (and your stove whose circuit board fried after a year), always opt for reliable brands that favor simplicity over fancy features. Weigh the costs and benefits of some harebrained Smart Can Opener. *It's ok to say no to new technology.* Marketers want us to believe that we can't live without The Next Big Thing. You know, things like... Smartwatches[78], Brother Power Note, CueCats, Google Glass, WebTV, the Pontiac Aztek, Windows Vista, Windows 8, Windows 10... You have the power to vote with your dollar, to avoid cloud services, and to reward makers of simple and reliable equipment. Make sure you know what you're getting into, and avoid proprietary platforms that will be obsoleted in a few years. You have the power to stop the madness.

Conclusion

Hipsters selling all-natural foods and old-fashioned record players give me hope (except the ones with the weird piercings). At least somebody out there believes in no-nonsense products that are designed to last.

I know my ideas here may seem radical and cynical, but I've discovered minimalism has led to happy customers and more success. Teknosophy's goal is informing, empowering, and thus liberating people. Sure, a handful of nerds may enjoy having a product that changes every day, but the vast majority of consumers, with whom I have all of my experience serving, simply want *consistency*.

You might now share my shock that such systemic injustice happens, often to the most vulnerable among us. I thought I'd grow up to invent something cutting-edge, but I now make my living selling two simple things: First, protection from technology that constantly breaks, and second, the revolutionary concept that the products you buy should actually be designed with care. The discovery and collection of these concepts has been frustrating (let's hope I sell enough books to afford hairplugs), but the explanation of them is my calling in life, and I'm proud to be the first to deliver this to you.

If you like what you've read, and are afflicted with some of these issues, I will soon begin authorizing independent technicians to perform cleanups with the Teknosophy method. That first new-customer makeover is the best! If you're part of an organization, you can contact me to schedule a speaking engagement. Thanks for reading! I hope you've enjoyed our time together, and consider buying a copy of the book for your friends!

Appendices

Further Reading

Books

Why Software Sucks, David Platt
The Cathedral and the Bazaar, Eric S. Raymond
Dune and *Dune Messiah*, Frank Herbert

Websites

The Register, British IT news
http://theregister.co.uk

Open Rights Group: Digital Rights Management
https://wiki.openrightsgroup.org/wiki/Digital_Rights_Management

Steve Jobs: Thoughts on Music
http://www.apple.com/kr/hotnews/thoughtsonmusic/

Sony Corporate History
http://www.sony.net/SonyInfo/CorporateInfo/History/history.html

Electronic Frontier Foundation
https://www.eff.org/issues/net-neutrality

Why China's Quantum Satellite Is Incredible—And Will Surely Be Overhyped
http://motherboard.vice.com/read/so-china-just-launched-a-quantum-satellite

Movies

Pirates of Silicon Valley (1999)
Jobs (2013)
The Code (2001)
Gattaca (1997)
Office Space (1999)
Terminator: Genisys (2015)
The Big Short (2015)

Glossary of Terms

419 scams Someone emails you to declare you've inherited money, intending to take yours

AdwCleaner Scanner that hunts for legal spyware such as toolbars and fake cleaners

App store A centralized software retailer website that reviews each product's integrity to ensure your safety

Autocorrect Feature of computers and phones that makes assumptions in an attempt to correct misspellings

Bitcoin Untraceable, decentralized, anational digital currency

Bloatware Legal software placed on a computer at the factory, to differentiate/advertise/slow down a machine

Blog Short for "web log", an online journal written by an independent writer

Bluetooth A wireless technology that allows computers, smartphones, cars, home stereos, mobile devices, video games, and accessories to talk to each other

Central Processing Unit (CPU) A powerful calculator made of silicon

Cloud The symbolic term referring to any Internet-based service

Cloudbook A super-cheap, stripped down laptop that's mainly only good for visiting websites

Combo boxes A combination of a modem and a router that does both jobs poorly

Cookies Small files that contain information about what web pages you've seen

Crowdfunding Asking friends to donate to a cause online

Crowdsourcing A platform whose users create the content to share with each other

Cryptolocker ransomware Unstoppable new-style malware that scrambles every document and photo you have

Daemons Programs that legally "haunt" your computer and slow it down, usually without your knowledge

Defragging Organizes new files so the computer can find them more easily

Digital cleansing Flushing records of your online activity

Digitally liquid Media that's easily transferred from one device to another

Distribution platforms A method of sharing content, such as YouTube

DNS tells your computer what IP address a website resides on

Driver is a small piece of software that teaches your Operating System how to deal with your particular accessory

DRM (Digital Rights Management or Digital Restrictions Management) A piracy-prevention program that requires buyers of legal downloads to request permission every time they use the product.

Dynamic IP Address An IP address that changes every time you reboot your modem or device

e-Commerce Websites where small businesses can sell to the world

Email worms Viruses that spread themselves through email

Encryption Swapping each letter in my message for another character, in order to conceal a message from all except the recipients who hold a key

Fake cleaners Programs that claim your computer is slow because of something irrelevant, then ask you for money

Firewall A passive filter that helps stop crank callers from sending commands to your computer

Hacker Can be an enthusiast who likes to tinker with technology, or a digital vandal

POP An antiquated email protocol that throws emails at your computer, rather than holding them in a server

IMAP An email protocol that implies a central email server holding your mail for you

Handshake A piece of software embedded in a media player that asks if the device is authorized to play that particular content

HDCP (High-Bandwidth Digital Content Protection) Anti-piracy technology embedded in home theater cabling

Helper overlay A more complex "shortcut" way to use the machine

Hostageware Locks your entire PC, runs a fake virus scan, and asks for money

IoT Internet of Things - Small post-computer devices that can perform small tasks while connected to the Internet

IP address A "phone number" or numerical name for any device connected to the Internet

ISP Internet Service Provider

Kill switches The ability to remotely disable something with the touch of a button

LibreOffice A free, open source clone of Microsoft's Office

Mail client A software program that allows you to read/write/organize your email messages

Malware Malicious software that enters a computer without the user's knowledge, to spy or damage it

Memes Inside jokes shared among Internet users

Metadata digital details collected about people's habits

Modem (modulator-demodulator) Converts information for transmittal along a wire, such as a telephone or cable wire

Motherboard is the main circuit board that ties it all together

Narrowcasting Broadcasting over the Internet, targeting a niche audience

NAS (Network Attached Storage) A hard drive with an Ethernet jack on the back, accessible by any computer in your building

Net Neutrality The argument that Internet providers have no right to peer into what you're doing and charge you based on that

Online cloud backup service is a one-lane one-way street that backs up your machine automatically throughout the day

Open Source Software written by volunteers, released as public domain, for the betterment of humanity

Operating System (OS) The main piece of software on your computer that allows you to run programs, such as Windows, Mac OSX, and Mint

P2P networks A network that introduces people to each other for the purpose of exchanging digital files

Phishing Receiving a fake email that claims to be from someone else

Platform agnostic created for all three of the major platforms, or without regard to any specific platform.

Power supply Takes electricity from your wall and distributes digestible portions of it to the components inside your computer

Print head The part of an inkjet printer that writes onto the paper

Private IP The number your devices go by while underneath a given router

Public IP The number your building (household, office, hospital, etc.) shows to the outside world

Quantum computers Computers made out of subatomic particles that eclipses current computers

Random access memory (RAM) It is not where your files are stored, rather, it is the scratch paper or cocktail napkin that your computer uses to do math

Rootkits Malware that hides in the "basement" of your computer

Router The appliance responsible for doling out your Internet connection to each device in a building

Skeuomorphs Icons based on real life, such as shopping carts, floppy disk save buttons, or telephone handset icons

Social Engineering Tricking a user emotionally

Software A computer program created so that a computer can perform a task, such as a game or a business bookkeeping program

Spyware The general term for software that lurks in your computer, monitors your behavior, and reports it to someone

Static IP Address An IP address that stays the same even after a reboot

Stowaway Software that comes in legally by paying to sneak in underneath another product

Support Scammers People who claim to be computer experts, scare you with fake virus scans, then ask for hundreds of dollars

Synchronization service allows me to synchronize the contents of all my personal computers

The New Threats The new threats that are occurring: Update Attacks, Legal Malware, Unstoppable Hostageware & Cryptolocker, and Support Scams

Toolbars Evil legal programs that hijack your homepage and screen space, intercept your Web searches, and reap data from your behaviors

Unix An Operating System that runs on servers

Update attacks Software improvements or patches that badger users relentlessly and sometimes damage products, all in the name of security

UPnP (called Bonjour in the Apple world) Searching for and summoning devices on a network by a fixed number

User Account Control (User Annoyance Control) Darkens your computer screen and plays a loud noise, then asks you for technical information

User data/home folder The stuff relevant to you, such as your desktop items, documents, photos, downloads, music, pictures, and videos

Vendor lock-in A vertical integration scheme that requires a customer to buy all accessories and all future products from the same company

VoIP (Voice over IP) A telephone line that carries your voice over the Internet

Web 2.0 Webites that allow reader participation

Web browser A software program that allows you to visit websites and read their content

Works Cited

1
Softonic: The Windows Store is full of fraudulent apps and Microsoft Doesn't Care
http://news.en.softonic.com/the-windows-store-is-full-of-scam-apps-and-microsoft-doesnt-care

2
Wikipedia: Seattle Computer Products
https://en.wikipedia.org/wiki/Seattle_Computer_Products

3
Wikipedia: Bill Gates
https://en.wikipedia.org/wiki/Bill_Gates

4
Microsoft: Tablets are a passing fad
http://www.mondaynote.com/2011/04/03/microsoft-tablets-are-a-passing-fad/

5
YouTube: Steve Jobs Insult Response
https://www.youtube.com/watch?v=FF-tKLISfPE

6
Bloomberg: The Man Who Could Have Been Bill Gates
http://www.bloomberg.com/bw/stories/2004-10-24/the-man-who-could-have-been-bill-gates

7
Automobile Magazine: Lanciapalooza Arrivederci Lancia
http://www.automobilemag.com/features/magazine/1503-lanciapalooza-arrivederci-lancia/

8
Technical Knowledge: What's an Ubuntu?
https://technicalknowledge.wordpress.com/2011/02/20/whats-an-ubuntu/

9
Princeton University: Ken Thompson interview, 9/6/89
https://www.princeton.edu/~hos/mike/transcripts/thompson.htm

10
Wikipedia: Linus Torvalds
https://en.wikipedia.org/wiki/Linus_Torvalds

11
Ars Technica: How Linux was born, as told by Linus Torvalds himself

http://arstechnica.com/information-technology/2015/08/how-linux-was-born-as-told-by-linus-torvalds-himself/

12
Wikipedia: Linus Torvalds Image (CC license)
https://upload.wikimedia.org/wikipedia/commons/6/69/Linus_Torvalds.jpeg

13
11 Apple iPads per hour vs. zero Microsoft Surface tablets
http://fortune.com/2012/11/26/11-apple-ipads-per-hour-vs-zero-microsoft-surface-tablets/

14
The Guardian: Kiss goodbye to your DRM-protected Google Video clips
http://www.theguardian.com/technology/2007/aug/16/guardianweeklytechnologysection.it

15
Wikipedia: Post Office Protocol
https://en.wikipedia.org/wiki/Post_Office_Protocol

16
Sony eBook Store
http://ebookstore.sony.com/downpage/index_b.html

17
The Register: RIAA Sues the Dead
http://www.theregister.co.uk/2005/02/05/riaa_sues_the_dead/

18
Steve Jobs: Thoughts on Music
http://www.apple.com/kr/hotnews/thoughtsonmusic/

19
From Netscape to Napster: Whatever happened to yesterday's giants?
http://www.pcworld.com/article/2067006/from-netscape-to-napster-whatever-happened-to-yesterdays-giants-.html

20
Wikipedia: Microsoft PlaysForSure
https://en.wikipedia.org/wiki/Microsoft_PlaysForSure

21
ORG Wiki: DVD DRM
https://wiki.openrightsgroup.org/wiki/Digital_Rights_Management#DVD_DRM

22

Amazon: Generic Compatible Ink Cartridge Replacement for Brother LC-61
http://www.amazon.com/Generic-Compatible-Replacement-Brother-LC-61/dp/B004GEHTVY/ref=sr_1_9?ie=UTF8&qid=1452356433&sr=8-9&keywords=brother+ink

23
Dallas News: HP Wants you to pay monthly
http://www.dallasnews.com/business/technology/20140109-hp-wants-you-to-pay-monthly-to-print--and-maybe-you-should.ece

24
HP Forums: How do I disable the Cartridge Protection
http://h30434.www3.hp.com/t5/Inkjet-Printing/How-do-I-disable-the-cartridge-protection-on-my-printer-HP/td-p/2510361

25
HP Accused of Expiring Ink Cartridges
https://www.techdirt.com/articles/20050222/1220232.shtml

26
New Genuine HP Cartridge not recognized
http://h30434.www3.hp.com/t5/Inkjet-Printing/New-genuine-HP-Cartridge-not-recognized/td-p/2380543

27
Wikipedia: IPv6
https://en.wikipedia.org/wiki/IPv6

28
NY Times: Internet Customers Surpass Cable Subscribers at Comcast
http://www.nytimes.com/2015/05/05/business/media/comcasts-earnings-rise-10-driven-by-high-speed-internet.html?_r=0

29
eBay: Brother Super Power Note Photo

30
Knowyourmeme.com: Memes

31
Gizmodo: Bluetooth is named after a medieval king who may have had a blue tooth
http://factually.gizmodo.com/bluetooth-is-named-after-a-medieval-king-who-may-have-h-1671450657

32
Arthur Rosenfeld: "Tai Chi: The Perfect Exercise"

33
Photo: Ken Thompson & Dennis Ritchie with President Clinton
http://www.quotationof.com/ken-thompson.html

34
Jalopnik article:
http://jalopnik.com/toyota-halts-production-at-three-plants-after-explosion-1780309156?google_editors_picks=true

35
Computerworld customer wins 10k
http://www.computerworld.com/article/3089071/microsoft-windows/customer-wins-10k-judgement-from-microsoft-over-unauthorized-windows-10-upgrade.html

36
Sony Corporate History
http://www.sony.net/SonyInfo/CorporateInfo/History/SonyHistory/1-03.html

37
Marketingland: Apple iPhone Drives Half Of All Mobile Internet Traffic
http://marketingland.com/report-apple-iphone-drives-half-mobile-internet-traffic-111129

38
Photo: Gates and Ballmer
http://latimesblogs.latimes.com/.a/6a00d8341c630a53ef014e6045c9fd970c-800wi

39
Photo: Steve Jobs and Steve Wozniak in 1977
http://vaultmg.com/wp-content/uploads/2014/12/steve-jobs-and-wozniak-1977.jpg

40
Tizen website
http://tizen.org/

41
Samsung Sued in China for Unremovable Bloatware
http://www.patentlyapple.com/patently-apple/2015/07/samsung-sued-in-china-for-unremovable-bloatware.html

42
Tech-Faq: How to Turn Off Real Message Center
http://www.tech-faq.com/how-to-turn-off-real-message-center.html

43
Malwarebytes Forums: ASPCA We-care
https://forums.malwarebytes.org/index.php?/topic/111991-what-is-this/

44
Business Insider: Steve Wozniak: Cloud Computing will cause Horrible Problems
http://www.businessinsider.com/steve-wozniak-cloud-computing-will-cause-horrible-problems-in-the-next-five-years-2012-8

45
PCMag: Wozniak warns against ditching iPhone headphone jack
http://www.pcmag.com/news/347279/wozniak-warns-against-ditching-iphone-headphone-jack

46
Huffington Post: Sneak Attack: Those Annoying Toolbars You Never Wanted
http://www.huffingtonpost.com/gary-m-kaye/sneak-attack-those-annoyi_b_4444859.html

47
Adobe Forum: Disable automatic updates in Adobe Reader DC?
https://forums.adobe.com/thread/1809982

48
Techdirt article: Stupidity Installing Bloatware That No One Uses Everyone Hates
https://www.techdirt.com/articles/20140423/15401627009/stupidity-installing-bloatware-that-no-one-uses-everyone-hates.shtml

49
Computerworld: Microsoft claims 200m Windows 8 licenses sold, but how many are in use?
http://www.computerworld.com/article/2487826/microsoft-windows/microsoft-claims-200m-windows-8-licenses-sold--but-how-many-are-in-use-.html

50
Autoblog: Gearheads Push to Preserve Right
http://www.autoblog.com/2015/05/08/gearheads-push-preserve-right-work-on-their-cars/

51
Gizmodo: In the Shower Eating Cherries
http://gizmodo.com/in-the-shower-eating-cherries-and-more-tales-of-night-1702059866

52
Bloomberg: US Widens Probe of Car Radios that May Be Vulnerable to Hacks
http://www.bloomberg.com/news/articles/2015-08-01/u-s-widens-probe-of-car-radios-that-may-be-vulnerable-to-hacks

53

Computerworld: Hack to steal cars with keyless ignition
http://www.computerworld.com/article/2971826/cybercrime-hacking/hack-to-steal-cars-with-keyless-ignition-volkswagen-spent-2-years-hiding-flaw.html

54
Screenshots taken myself. All programs are property of their respective owners.

55
Botcrawl: How to remove MyPCBackup
http://botcrawl.com/how-to-remove-mypc-backup/

56
Photo of Mark Shuttleworth: Wikipedia
https://upload.wikimedia.org/wikipedia/commons/7/78/Mark_Shuttleworth_by_Martin_Schmitt.jpg

57
DailyTech: Apple's Maps App Flunks at Geography, Navigation
http://www.dailytech.com/Quick+Note+Apples+Maps+App+Flunks+at+Geography+Navigation/article24926.htm

58
Scientific American: In Tech We Don't Trust

59
Arstechnica.com: Are comcast's Arris modem/wifi combos universally bad?
http://arstechnica.com/civis/viewtopic.php?t=1256475

60
HP issues non-apology for blocking third-party ink cartridges
https://techcrunch.com/2016/09/29/hp-issues-non-apology-for-blocking-third-party-ink-cartridges/

61
Six Colors: Syncing feeling: iCloud Drive in macOS Sierra
https://sixcolors.com/post/2016/10/sierra-icloud-drive/

62
Reuters: U.S. warns on Java software as security concerns escalate
http://www.reuters.com/article/us-java-security-idUSBRE90A0S320130111

63
CBS: New scam holds your computer files for ransom
http://www.cbsnews.com/news/new-scam-holds-your-computer-files-for-ransom/

64
Gizmodo: Former Facebook Workers: We Routinely Suppressed Conservative News

http://gizmodo.com/former-facebook-workers-we-routinely-suppressed-conser-1775461006

65
NPR: 'Internet Of Things' Hacking Attack Led To Widespread Outage Of Popular Websites
http://www.npr.org/2016/10/22/498954197/internet-outage-update-internet-of-things-hacking-attack-led-to-outage-of-popula

66
Stephen Hawking warns artificial intelligence could end mankind
http://www.bbc.com/news/technology-30290540

67
Everalbum is proof that SMS invite spam still works
https://techcrunch.com/2016/09/21/everalbum-is-proof-that-sms-spam-still-works/

68
Backupreview: MyPCBackup
http://www.backupreview.com/mypcbackup-justcloud-zipcloud/

69
TrendLabs Security Intelligence Blog: New DYRE Variant Hijacks Microsoft Outlook, Expands Targeted Banks
http://blog.trendmicro.com/trendlabs-security-intelligence/new-dyre-variant-hijacks-microsoft-outlook-expands-targeted-banks/

70
Vice: Government Must Prepare for When Quantum Computers Can Crack Its Encryption
http://motherboard.vice.com/read/NIST-quantum-computers-can-crack-its-encryption-RSA

71
Little known search engine that refuses to store data on users doubles web traffic amid NSA tapping scandal
http://www.dailymail.co.uk/news/article-2360059/DuckDuckGo-little-known-search-engine-refuses-store-data-users-doubles-web-traffic-amid-NSA-tapping-scandal.html

72
How to remove the Windows 10 GWX upgrade nonsense
http://www.dedoimedo.com/computers/windows-7-to-10-gwx-how-to-remove.html

73
Cory Doctorow: "How Laws Restricting Tech Actually Expose Us to Greater Harm"
https://www.wired.com/2014/12/government-computer-security/

74
A New Wireless Hack Can Unlock 100 Million Volkswagens
https://www.wired.com/2016/08/oh-good-new-hack-can-unlock-100-million-volkswagens/

75
Yahoo says hackers stole data from 500 million accounts in 2014
http://www.reuters.com/article/us-yahoo-cyber-idUSKCN11S16P

76
Wikipedia: LibreOffice
https://en.wikipedia.org/wiki/LibreOffice

77
Apple Communities: Viruses, Trojans, Malware - and other aspects of Internet Security
https://discussions.apple.com/docs/DOC-3028

78
Businses Insider: Wearables are Dead
http://www.businessinsider.com/wearables-are-dead-2016-12

79
App Store users can bring antitrust lawsuit against Apple
https://www.cnet.com/news/app-store-users-can-bring-an-antitrust-lawsuit-against-apple/?google_editors_picks=true

80
Samsung's Note7 kill switch: Who really owns your phone?
http://mashable.com/2016/12/09/galaxy-note-7-nanny-state/#Iv_jFlnbrgqV

81
Google Search – windows installer service stopped working
https://www.google.com/search?q=windows+installer+service+stopped+working

82
Microsoft: Buy Microsoft Office 365 Home & Personal subscriptions
https://products.office.com/en-US/buy/office

83
Quartz Media: Your brilliant Kickstarter idea could be on sale in China before you've even finished funding it (Open Source Manufacturing section)
https://qz.com/771727/chinas-factories-in-shenzhen-can-copy-products-at-breakneck-speed-and-its-time-for-the-rest-of-the-world-to-get-over-it/

84
Business Insider: 'Total amateur hour': Hillary Clinton's private server seemed shockingly vulnerable
http://www.businessinsider.com/total-amateur-hour-hillary-clintons-private-server-seemed-shockingly-hackable-2015-10

85
Ars Technica: Vizio smart TVs tracked viewers around the clock without consent
https://arstechnica.com/tech-policy/2017/02/vizio-smart-tvs-tracked-viewers-around-the-clock-without-consent/

86
Netflix to FCC: reclassify Comcast and Verizon so they can't choke the internet
https://gigaom.com/2014/07/16/netflix-to-fcc-reclassify-comcast-and-verizon-so-they-cant-choke-the-internet/

87
Google search: "Outlook corrupted"
https://www.google.com/search?q=outlook+corrupted

About the Author

Marc-Anthony Arena was born in the 80s, back when technology was hopeful.

He attended the all-boys McQuaid Jesuit High School, and then the mostly-boys Rochester Institute of Technology, where he majored in Business Management with concentrations in Entrepreneurship, Spanish, and Russian. There, he co-founded a juice bar and a local chapter of Sigma Alpha Epsilon.

Marc has worked in the IT industry since 2000, and is currently President and Founder of both Teknosophy, LLC, and Streamplicity. He is also the host of "The Computer Exorcist Show" on WYSL Radio, available on AM, FM, and online.

In his free time, he enjoys funny Internet videos, roadtrips down the Eastern Seaboard, cigars, Tai Chi, foreign languages, buying old convertibles, and paying dearly for their repairs.

By the time you read this, he should have retired to the Italian countryside. There, he'll eat lamb every day, and never have to touch another computer again.